D0053352

BEFORE YOU
HIT SEND

BEFORE YOU

HIT

SEND

PREVENTING HEADACHE AND HEARTACHE

Emerson Eggerichs, PhD

W PUBLISHING GROUP

AN IMPRINT OF THOMAS NELSON

Published in Nashville, Tennessee, by W Publishing Group, an imprint of Thomas Nelson.

Thomas Nelson titles may be purchased in bulk for educational, business, fund-raising, or sales promotional use. For information, please e-mail SpecialMarkets@ThomasNelson.com.

Unless otherwise noted, Scripture quotations are taken from New American Standard Bible®. © 1960, 1962, 1963, 1968, 1971, 1972, 1973, 1975, 1977, 1995 by The Lockman Foundation. Used by permission.

Scripture quotation marked CEV is from the Contemporary English Version. © 1991, 1992, 1995 by American Bible Society. Used by permission.

Scripture quotation marked GW is from *God's Word*®. © 1995 God's Word to the Nations. Used by permission of Baker Publishing Group. All rights reserved.

Scripture quotation marked NIrV is from the Holy Bible, New International Reader's Version®, NIrV®. © 1995, 1996, 1998, 2014 by Biblica, Inc.® Used by permission of Zondervan. All rights reserved worldwide.

Scripture quotations marked NIV are from the Holy Bible, New International Version®, NIV®. © 1973, 1978, 1984, 2011 by Biblica, Inc.® Used by permission of Zondervan. All rights reserved worldwide.

Scripture quotation marked NLT is from the Holy Bible, New Living Translation. © 1996, 2004, 2007, 2013, 2015 by Tyndale House Foundation. Used by permission of Tyndale House Publishers, Inc., Carol Stream, Illinois 60188. All rights reserved.

Italics and other emphases added to Scripture quotations are the author's own.

Names and facts from stories contained in this book have been changed, but the sentiments expressed are true as related to the author through personal conversations, letters, or e-mails. Permission has been granted for the use of real names, stories, and correspondence.

ISBN 978-0-7180-9540-6 (eBook)

Library of Congress Cataloging-in-Publication Data

Names: Eggerichs, Emerson, author.
Title: Before you hit send : preventing headache and heartache / Emerson
    Eggerichs, PhD.
Description: Nashville : W Publishing Group, 2017.
Identifiers: LCCN 2017003530 | ISBN 9780718094263 (hardback)
Subjects: LCSH: Social media—Moral and ethical aspects. | Online social
    networks—Moral and ethical aspects.
Classification: LCC HM741 .E44 2017 | DDC 302.23/1—dc23 LC record available at https://
lccn.loc.gov/2017003530

My two grandchildren—Jackson, 6, and Ada, 2—bring Sarah ("Mimi") and me ("Poppi") such deep delight. We have a saying chalked and framed, "Grand-parenting is the only thing in life that is not over-rated."

But when I envision their future, should any of us underrate the world they will inherit? How will they navigate their interactions with the people of the earth? We all know most cultures will be at their fingertips—literally, in e-mails, texts, tweets, and so on. They will be able to communicate with anyone, anywhere, through Skyping or FaceTime.

Therefore, I dedicate this book to Jackson and Ada Joy Marie to help guide their thoughts and words. This book challenges them to think before they speak and reminds them to think about four questions before speaking: Is it true? Kind? Necessary? And clear?

If the answer is no, do not hit send.

If the answer is yes, Poppi says, "Hit send!"

CONTENTS

TRUE, KIND, NECESSARY, AND CLEAR: THE FOOTBALL OF COMMUNICATION

Dance like no one is watching; email like it may one day be read aloud in a deposition.

—Olivia Nuzzi, *The Daily Beast*

This telling quote, by Olivia Nuzzi of *The Daily Beast*, came out on the heels of the hack of nearly twenty thousand e-mails of the Democratic National Committee, prior to their national convention in 2016.[1]

Every twenty-four hours, 205 billion e-mails are sent across cyberspace;[2] every sixty seconds, 510 comments are posted on Facebook (that's 734,000 posts per day);[3] and every second, almost six thousand tweets are tweeted across the Internet for the entire Twitterverse to see, totaling 350,000 tweets per minute and 500 million tweets per day.[4]

Though the head spins with these statistics, they do not include those going out through YouTube, LinkedIn, Pinterest, Google Plus, Tumblr, Instagram, or the countless other platforms being created every year. Would it be safe then to say that out of these hundreds of billions of communications each and every day, large numbers of the contents' authors wish they had taken the time to think more carefully about all they were communicating and revised, or even deleted entirely, the messages they sent out recklessly in an emotional moment?

When it happens to you, a family member, or an employee, you understand the anguish it can cause and how relevant this becomes.

What about the athlete who cannot help but post all his opinions toward the league or team he plays for, perhaps not realizing that freedom of speech does not mean there can't be consequences from his employer?

Or the politician who has media and watchdog organizations analyzing every comment she makes, not hesitating to take their presumptions public with what they believe the candidate is communicating?

Or the television personality who is quick to post controversial opinions that are not received well by the general public, causing so much uproar and backlash that suspension or even termination becomes necessary?

But one doesn't have to be in the public limelight to regret an e-mail or social media post. Take, for example, the job applicant for a major software company who tweeted that she was just offered a job, but now she had to **weigh the utility of a fatty paycheck against the daily commute to San Jose and hating the work.** Shortly after her not-well-thought-through tweet, she received a reply from an employee at the firm who was seeking to hire her, asking her, **Who is the hiring manager? I'm sure they would love to know that you will hate the work. We here at Cisco are versed in the web.**[5]

Justine Sacco was global head of communications for a media conglomerate, living in New York and flying home to South Africa for Christmas, when she tweeted, **Going to Africa. Hope I don't get AIDS. Just kidding. I'm white!** After the plane touched down, she learned that her tweet had gone viral, the outcome of which was that her employer fired her and she underwent unthinkable hostility.[6]

Sacco sent what she considered a ridiculous, over-the-top, ironic tweet. But it wasn't received that way. She quickly became the poster child for bad tweets, and the incident was covered widely.

Social media means what it says: it is *social*. World Wide Web means worldwide. Our methods of communication today allow our message to be broadcast to potentially millions, from Auckland, New Zealand, to Oakland, California. But it's not only Twitter fanatics who can find themselves in trouble. Every single one of us could fall prey, especially with e-mail. That's why author Seth Godin always asks himself before hitting send in an e-mail, "Is there anything in this e-mail that I don't want the attorney general, the media or my boss seeing? (If so, hit delete.)"[7]

Checklists and questions like these help in all forms of communication, not just with e-mail and social media. I'll bet Tony, who wrote the following on the Love and Respect Facebook page, wishes he had gone through a mental checklist before putting his foot in his mouth while at work:

> Once, while working customer service at the meat counter, I asked a mother with a toddler and a rather protruding stomach area, "When is the baby due?" She informed me she wasn't pregnant. Catching my mistake, I countered with, "No, I mean, when is the

baby due for kindergarten?" Referring to the toddler. By her expression she didn't buy it. From then on I learned to listen more before opening my mouth.

Or the pastor who announced from the pulpit one week, "Come next week and listen to our new organ player play and find out what hell is really like." He didn't think before speaking! Instead, his lips got ahead of his brain as he tried promoting both the new organist and his sermon on hell. He didn't ask quickly enough, "How is this going to be heard?"

Every day we have the potential of both verbal and written blunders. It makes no difference if we are talking to a stranger over a meat counter, chatting on a cell phone with the service department, or sending an e-mail to a coworker; we can miscommunicate and people can get the wrong idea.

When we don't stop to think before we speak, we increase the odds that we will misrepresent our best selves, which could result in people misinterpreting us. We leave them wondering if we have goodwill or good sense, or neither. When we speak before we think, we widen the chances the other person(s) will be notably hurt, frustrated, confused, angry, fearful, or offended by something we've communicated.

And things can go south quickly

- during a face-to-face conversation on Skype with our mothers, who are upset that we don't communicate regularly;
- in a text exchange with a landscaper who didn't show up to work on the lawn;
- at a table during a Sunday church potluck when the styles of worship music are hotly debated;
- at a management meeting with fellow workers disgruntled over no bonuses this year;
- during an interview with a future employer who questions our credentials; or
- in a series of tweets we send to neighbors about our favorite political candidate who they view as Satan's relative.

Though the title of the book is *Before You Hit Send*, implying the importance of thinking through all the possible consequences of your tweet, e-mail, or Facebook post before hitting "send," the true maxim the title represents is "Think before you speak."

And what exactly should you "think before you speak"? Here are four questions to ask yourself with everything you communicate:

- Is it true?
- Is it kind?
- Is it necessary?
- Is it clear?

⁓

As a college student, I sat in a chapel service at Wheaton College and heard a speaker make the following statement: "All of us must ask three questions before communicating: Is it true, kind, and necessary?" I don't remember the name or face of that speaker, but I remember that advice as though it was given yesterday. It rang true for me immediately. I never had to memorize it. That brief sentence struck a chord and stuck in my brain. It was an unforgettable, life-changing moment. Hearing that comment chaperoned my thinking for more than four decades.

I learned later that many have credited Socrates, the philosopher who lived from 469 to 399 BC, with the vital importance of asking, "Is it true, is it kind, or is it necessary?"[8] No one knows, however, who penned the exact question. I asked a friend of mine who is a professor of philosophy if he could direct me to the exact quote from Socrates, and he replied, "You stump me on that one." I asked my good friend Eric Metaxes, who founded Socrates in the City in Manhattan, and he e-mailed back,

I just did a Google search, and it's pretty inconclusive, honestly.

Regardless, in that chapel service I came into the possession of a rule of communication that has worked well for me (and will for you). Each concept has guided and guarded my speech and writing, and many others have testified to the richness of this wisdom.

In *The Children's Story Garden* from 1920, we read about "The Three Sieves":

> A little boy one day ran indoors from school and called out eagerly, "Oh, mother, what do you think of Tom Jones? I have just heard that—"
>
> "Wait a minute, my boy. Have you put what you have heard through the three sieves before you tell it to me?"
>
> "Sieves, mother! What do you mean?"
>
> "Well, the first sieve is called Truth. Is it true?"
>
> "Well, I don't really know, but Bob Brown said that Charlie told him that Tom—"
>
> "That's very roundabout. What about the second sieve—Kindness. Is it kind?"
>
> "Kind! No, I can't say it is kind."
>
> "Now the third sieve—Necessity. Will it go through that? Must you tell this tale?"
>
> "No, mother, I need not repeat it."

"Well, then, my boy, if it is not necessary, not kind, and perhaps not true, let the story die."[9]

What I do know is that these three ideas pulsate in the Bible. Who does not quote Ephesians 4:15, which states, "Speak the truth in love" (NLT)? There we have truth and kindness. As a pastor for nearly twenty years, I often heard that verse roll off the lips of folks in my congregation.

Or who has not quoted, or at least heard quoted, Ecclesiastes 3:7, "A time to be silent and a time to speak"? Some things aren't necessary to say and some things are. We may not have known the exact reference for the verse, but the truth made a lasting impression.

Bottom line, we intuitively know that we ought to speak the truth in love at the appropriate time. We recognize this as a foundational aspect of interpersonal communication. It rings true for all of us.

This appealed to me since I never wanted people to say to me, "What you just said is untrue, unkind, and un-necessary." To be criticized that way would be a rebuke that would deeply disturb my soul. Instead, I wished to be a person whom, when I spoke or wrote, others would view as accurate, goodwilled, and helpful. I had a desire to be competent, trustworthy, and effective. I wanted to be a good communicator. I did not want headaches and heart-aches because I was forever speaking before thinking.

"But, Emerson, didn't you list four questions for everyone to ask themselves?" Yes, since that day in the chapel service, I have come to the conclusion that a fourth checklist item must be added to true, kind, and necessary: what we are communicating to another must also be clear.

There were many times I knew that what I said was true, kind, and necessary but later found out that I had been unclear.

For example, I wrongly assumed others knew all the facts—the whole *truth*. But as they were not up to speed, they felt in the dark and confused about what I communicated.

I assumed people understood that I was being silly in my comment, not sarcastic and *unkind*. Instead, they thought I belittled them.

I assumed the readers appreciated all the information but found out soon enough they deemed some of it *unnecessary* since it confused them and they had to ask, "What exactly is your point?"

The apostle Paul asserted this need to be clear. We read in 1 Corinthians 14:9, "Unless you utter by the tongue speech that is clear, how will it be known what is spoken?" This is a universally rhetorical question.

For me, when I put these four concepts in a checklist, good things happen.

- Is this communication true?
- Is this communication kind?
- Is this communication necessary?
- Is this communication clear?

I know these are vital. Why? Because I want you to talk to me this way! I do not want you to lie to me, be rude, tell me what I don't need to know, or leave me confused by hard-to-follow remarks.

I know that when I answer these four questions in my communication with you, it decreases the likelihood that you will get the wrong idea and increases the likelihood that you will get the right idea! It saves me a lot of time correcting misunderstandings and rupturing relationships. It prevents headaches and heartaches.

—

Years ago Robert Fulghum wrote a book called *All I Really Need to Know I Learned in Kindergarten.*[10] I love that title. It implies that by the time we were five years old, we had already learned enough to get us through life in a successful way interpersonally if only we'd act on it later as an adult!

To this point, who does not know the axiom "think before you speak"? Every father and mother told us this foundational principle in communication starting at age four if not before. But the wisest among us knows that there is no absolute guarantee that we will act today on what we know from yesterday.

When it comes to truly succeeding as a person who interacts with others, it isn't about learning new things as much as it is about acting on the wisdom of the ages we learned at age five. The basics are the basics for a reason.

In the book *When Pride Still Mattered: A Life of Vince Lombardi,* David Maraniss wrote about Lombardi in 1961 at the beginning of training camp for the Green Bay Packers:

> He took nothing for granted. He began a tradition of starting from scratch, assuming that the players were blank slates who carried over no knowledge from the year before. . . . He began with the most elemental statement of all. "Gentlemen," he said, holding a pigskin in his right hand, "this is a football."[11]

Let me tell you, the best of communicators need to remember the "football" every day.

For me, the football of communication is to always ask the four questions. When I do not, I drop the ball.

In the pages to come, I want us to return to the basics and look closely at these four concepts. We will answer the following questions:

- Is that which I'm about to say the truth, the whole truth, and nothing but the truth?
- Does it sound loving and respectful?
- Do I know if it should be said now, later, or at all?
- Is it clear to me and to the other person?

Let's dance like everyone is watching. Let's write like everyone is reading. Let's speak like everyone is listening.

CHAPTER 1

IS IT TRUE?

Scriptural Meditation on True Speech

- Ephesians 4:25—Therefore, laying aside falsehood, **speak truth** *each one* of you *with his neighbor*, for we are members of one another.
- Colossians 3:9—**Do not lie** to one another, since you laid aside the old self with its evil practices.
- Titus 1:2—**God . . . cannot lie**.
- Acts 5:3-4—But Peter said, "Ananias, why has Satan filled your heart to lie to the Holy Spirit and to keep back some of the price of the land? While it remained unsold, did it not remain your own? And after it was

sold, was it not under your control? Why is it that you have conceived this deed in your heart? **You have not lied to men but to God.**"

- Revelation 14:4-5—These are the ones who follow the Lamb wherever He goes. These have been purchased from among men as first fruits to God and to the Lamb. And **no lie was found in their mouth**; they are blameless.
- Proverbs 12:19—**Truthful lips** will be established forever, but a **lying tongue** is only for a moment.
- Proverbs 12:22—**Lying lips** are an abomination to the LORD, but those who deal faithfully are His delight.
- Proverbs 19:5—A **false witness** will not go unpunished, and he who tells lies will not escape.
- Proverbs 21:6—The acquisition of **treasures by a lying tongue is a fleeting vapor**, the pursuit of death.
- Psalm 35:20—For they do not speak peace, But they devise **deceitful words** against those who are quiet in the land.

Is It the Truth, the Whole Truth, and Nothing but the Truth, So Help You God?

In Charles Dickens's *Great Expectations*, we read, "'There's one thing you may be sure of, Pip,' said Joe, after some rumination, 'namely, that lies is lies. Howsever they come, they didn't ought to come.'"[1]

The US court system reveals three "howsever" of lies. Witnesses are asked, as they raise their right hands and place their left on a Bible, "Do you swear to tell the truth, the whole truth, and nothing but the truth, so help you God?"

Under threat of perjury, a person must avoid three ways to lie. First, do not communicate what we know or believe is false. That is not telling the truth. Second, do not communicate half truths. A half truth misleads. Third, do not pepper the whole truth with lies since it makes the whole truth uncertain.

Sadly, unless asked to take an oath under the penalty of perjury, some people are prone to lie. Human nature possesses this bent. A fellow e-mailed me, **Lying happens rampantly. I do it. Others do it. Seems everyone is lying. It's just easier to not tell the truth.** I suppose such folks do not find lying pleasant, only commonplace.

Once a witness is caught in a lie, the courts are done with that testimony. Who can believe people after they've been caught in a lie? In lying once on the stand, they've lied twice because earlier they swore to tell the truth. Even if they now tell the truth, the judge and jury do not trust them.

Some contend that it is okay to say things that are

untrue as long as we believe it is spoken out of necessity and kindness.

However, a lie is a lie by any other name, as a rose is a rose by any other name. No matter how compassionate one feels in telling the untruth, eventually someone exposes the lie.

The world-renowned medical researcher Dr. John Ioannidis has exposed the brightest and the best in academia. "His model predicted, in different fields of medical research, rates of wrongness . . . 80 percent of non-randomized studies (by far the most common type) turn out to be wrong, as do 25 percent of supposedly gold-standard randomized trials, and as much as 10 percent of the platinum-standard large randomized trials." Of the forty-nine top pieces of research that impacted the medical field unlike any other discoveries, and which were quoted countlessly around the world, thirty-four were retested, and fourteen of these were wrong! "These were articles that helped lead to the widespread popularity of treatments such as the use of hormone-replacement therapy for menopausal women, vitamin E to reduce the risk of heart disease, coronary stents to ward off heart attacks, and daily low-dose aspirin to control blood pressure and prevent heart attacks and strokes." Ioannidis believes "that researchers were frequently manipulating data analyses, chasing career-advancing findings rather than good science, and even using the peer-review process—in which journals ask researchers to help decide which studies to publish—to suppress opposing views."[2]

It makes no difference if our spin is compelled by our compassion or career advancement or the suppression of opposite positions; little good comes to us when we refuse to tell the truth, the whole truth, and nothing but the truth. Abraham Lincoln wrote, "Falsehood . . . is the worst enemy a fellow can have. The fact is truth is your truest friend, no matter what the circumstances are."[3]

The Heart of Communicating What Is True

In the 1800s, a young African in his early teens stood on a block of wood about to be auctioned off to the highest bidder among several slave owners. Before the bidding began, one of them approached him and asked, "If I buy you, will you be honest?" He replied respectfully, "I will be honest whether you buy me or not."[4]

When I heard someone tell that story years ago, I had an "Aha" moment. This young man's example profoundly affected my thinking. He would be honest independent of people and circumstances. He was an individual created in the image of God who had the freedom to live by God's moral code, and no one could make him do otherwise. He had decided to be a person of integrity. He may have been a slave, a victim of an evil incivility, but he refused to be a slave to lies. His incredible example caused me to conclude that other people do not cause me to lie but reveal my choice to be untruthful. This is a heart issue.

Jesus said, "For the mouth speaks out of that which fills the heart. The good man brings out of his good treasure what is good . . ." (Matt. 12:34–35). In other words, the mouth speaks what is good and honest because of a good heart. Though Jesus recognized the sinful and fallen condition of each person, and the need to trust Him as Savior, He did not hesitate in describing some people as having a "good heart." We read in Luke 8:15, "But the seed in the good soil, these are the ones who have heard the word in an honest and good heart, and hold it fast, and bear fruit with perseverance."

On the other hand, lying points to a bad heart—our darker nature. In John 8:44, Jesus said to the Pharisees, "You are of your father the devil, and you want to do the desires of your father. He . . . does not stand in the truth because there is no truth in him. Whenever he speaks a lie, he speaks from his own nature, for he is a liar and the father of lies."

According to Jesus, lying arises out of one's nature. By way of analogy, what do you have when a drunken horse thief decides to stop drinking? You have a horse thief. His nature to steal remains.

How do we know if lying is in our nature? We have our price, and we will lie when our price is met. In the Bible, Ananias wanted to make the same impression on the early church as did Barnabas (Acts 5). Barnabas sold a piece of property and gave all the money to the church. Ananias wanted to dazzle the new community in the same way. He yearned for the same recognition that Barnabas received. However, Ananias plotted a way to avoid the same sacrifice. He sold a piece of property for a certain amount, let's say $250,000 in today's economy. But he told church leaders he sold it for $150,000 and he was giving the full price to the church. The truth was he kept $100,000 for himself. Ananias compromised his integrity for a price, and as a result, God took his life, as well as the life of his wife, Sapphira, who had gone along with the lie.

Do we have a price? At what price would we compromise our character of integrity?

The Golden Rule of True Communication

I recently spoke with a friend who learned from a mechanic that his vehicle had a major problem, which made his car worthless. If my friend proceeded to have work done on the vehicle, the repair shop would need to record the car's previous ills on Carfax as part of the public record. The manager said, "Because of these repairs, people won't buy it once it goes on Carfax. On the other hand, if we don't do the work, you can sell it without the buyer knowing the serious problem since there will be no public record on Carfax." My friend asked what he should do. I replied, "Well, the answer is easy enough. If you were the consumer and someone withheld the truth about this car from you, you'd be up in arms when the car seized up and died on the highway during rush hour. I've found honesty is the best policy even if in the short-haul it proves more costly."

The Golden Rule says, "Treat others the same way you want them to treat you" (Luke 6:31). Want to know how to communicate truthfully each time? Ask yourself a variant of the Golden Rule: *Am I about to communicate unto others in the way I would want others to communicate unto me?*

What I find fascinating is that some people—some very smart people—compromise at this juncture. They want to be treated with the Golden Rule of true communication but do not want to be bound by it. They utterly ignore their hypocrisy. One of the great philosophers on conversation, Paul Grice, espoused various maxims on communication, such as "Do not say what you believe to be false." About these one academic wrote, "These maxims may be better understood as describing the assumptions listeners normally make about the way speakers will talk, rather than prescriptions for how one ought to talk . . . 'Although Grice presented them in the form of guidelines for how to communicate successfully . . . they are better construed as presumptions . . . that we as listeners rely on and as speakers exploit' (Bach 2005)."[5]

Did you catch the point? When others speak to us, we expect them to be truthful; but when we speak to them, we reserve the option to lie. In other words, don't lie to me but I can lie to you. Are we that much more important than others?

When push comes to shove, and we feel telling the truth will cause us to lose something or not gain something, do we give wrong information to protect our interests? Do we hedge on the truth and mislead people? Do we buckle and compromise the truth? Do we fail to say what we know is the right thing to say? Or are we committed to doing what we know is right: to tell the truth, the whole truth, and nothing but the truth, so help us God?

If we know that truthful communication should be a two-way street, why in the world would we reject the Golden Rule of true communication and lie to others when we expect them to be true to us? Let's consider several "reasons."

Why Do We Communicate What Is Untrue?

Years ago a friend asked me, "Do you know the meaning of rationalize? Rational lies." This insight captures a great deal of truth about why we are untrue. We have our reasons!

The difficulty is that many times we do think before we speak (or hit send); we want to communicate the truth, but we let other factors change our minds. Here I invite you to consider twenty rational lies. Do any of these ring true to you? Is this the inner script you speak to yourself and others about why you are less than truthful at times? Let's address each briefly.

THE FEARFUL: Honestly, I dread the consequences
over past missteps, so I cover them up.

THE SELFISH: What can I say? Lying works to my
advantage, advancing my agenda.

THE EVASIVE: If others don't know what I did
wrong, there'll be fewer problems all around.

THE PRIDEFUL: I need to look better than I am so
others will feel good about me and like me.

THE EXPEDIENT: I lie since it is quicker and easier for
me at the moment.

THE EMOTIONAL: If it feels true, I say it. I don't need
all the facts when I feel I'm right.

THE INATTENTIVE: I didn't know that what I said was inaccurate; everyone makes mistakes.

THE FLATTERER: I want to be truthful plus tactful, but insincere praise works better for me.

THE SELF-DELUDED: Some claim I lie to myself. But that's a lie. I'm 100 percent honest with myself.

THE CHAMELEON: To duck conflict, I bend my beliefs to fit my audience, which pleases them.

THE ENTRAPPED: It's not my fault. I was lured into swearing secrecy and facilitated a lie.

THE PROTECTOR: I feel responsible to protect another's interests even if I have to lie to do so.

THE CHRONIC: I've always lied even when the truth was better. Something comes over me.

THE COPYCAT: I'm not really interested in lying, but everybody else lies, so I do too.

THE PERPETUATOR: I lie to stay out ahead of other lies I have told; sadly, lies beget lies.

THE ASHAMED: I'm a bit humiliated over the bad stuff I've done, so I lie to appear good.

THE OATH-MAKER: I admit, when hedging, I swear to God so others believe what I'm saying.

THE BRAINY: I'm smart, retaining both the lies and truth. It's easy to get away with lying.

THE WORDSMITH: I find it easy and fun to twist words, using double meanings that mislead.

THE SELF-AMUSER: Frankly, I view tricking others as an exciting and entertaining game.

The Fearful

Oftentimes we fear that disfavor will come upon us if we speak what is negatively true, either about ourselves or someone else. Fearful folks can remain silent about the truth. Or we could decide to say or do something at odds with the truth to prevent our fears from being realized. Observe how fear drives the following reasons for telling a lie?

- I lied about the affair because I was afraid my spouse would divorce me.
- If I don't lie about this new product on the company's website, I fear management's wrath.
- I lied about the proposal and the timeline by telling the potential client what they wanted to hear for fear they wouldn't hire me.
- I lied about my credentials on the résumé for fear they wouldn't give me an interview.
- I lied to my boss on the report because I feared conflict with her.
- I did not tell the whole truth when I tweeted about the candidate I hate for fear the whole truth would put him in a good light and help his election,

and he'd then enact laws at odds with my social interests.

- I lied on Facebook about the exotic trip to Asia for fear that people would not find me important and happy if they knew of my daily life.

The Selfish

A peer at work is up for the same promotion that you seek, and only one of you will get it. Unfortunately, the CEO asks if you are able to provide information to this peer on a certain project. If you do, you enable this peer to succeed and mar your chances for the advancement, so you feign ignorance. "Sorry, I don't have that information."

Or, perhaps, to gain the empathy from your girl-friends that is of colossal value to you, you tell only part of the story about the fight you had with your husband. You describe in detail what he did wrong and say nothing about what you did, which prompted his negative reaction.

We are all capable of manipulating information for self-serving purposes, telling others incorrect information to advance our interests, and suppressing those who might block our progress. When we want something badly enough, we are tempted to lie to gain it if we see an opportunity to get away with it.

Each of us must decide if forgoing the truth to get

what we want is the course we should take. Multiple Tour de France champion Lance Armstrong denied doping charges for all those years, and the public believed him. He rebutted the allegations in face-to-face interviews, on the phone with people, and through every social media outlet. He would defend himself with, "I never tested positive or was ever caught for anything."[6] Eventually, a fellow rider, Floyd Landis, confessed to the drugging on the US Postal Service team, and the rest is history. So why did Lance lie? He wanted to be number one at any price and convinced himself that because others drugged themselves too, this leveled the playing field. Yet he validated a Russian proverb: "With lies you may get ahead in the world—but you can never go back."[7]

In saying that we need to think before we speak, we should actually say, "*What* will we think before we speak?" Some of us think, *I need to lie to get what I want*, and we hit send.

The Evasive

We did something that was not good or acceptable, like used discretionary funds from the company to buy an expensive golf club driver. But we conclude if no one knows what we did, it will be better for all involved. "Why hurt my reputation and get others mad at me when what they don't know won't hurt them? No harm, no foul."

When finding ourselves in those situations where someone asks about the expenditures, we remain vague or plead ignorance. We are evasive. Yet, there come those moments of a near heart attack. A fellow worker comes into our office and says, "The CEO wants to see you." Immediately, we break out in a nervous sweat. Because we did not come clean on the misuse of those discretionary funds, which was pocket change compared to what the company makes, we have an anxiety attack. We feel the evasion is over. We feel caught. Our mouths dry up. We conclude the CEO intends to fire us. But wait, maybe we can come up with an excuse. Maybe we can evade the truth one more time. We quickly formulate the line that we intended to pay the company back for the money we used to buy the golf club but honestly we forgot to pay it back.

Upon entering his office, he says, "Hey, thanks. I have a quick comment and request. Good job on the Macintosh account. Excellent. Because of that, I want you to give a report on the account to the management team next Tuesday at ten a.m. here in my office."

As we leave the office, our sense of relief cannot be measured. Yet it is here we know the truth about our evasive lying. Our conscience speaks loud and clear: "People who walk in truth do not experience heart palpitations like this."

God provides the conscience to whisper, "Change

course. Be honest. Make things right." The person who comes clean realizes that it isn't just about him. Khaled Hosseini said in *The Kite Runner*, "When you tell a lie, you steal someone's right to the truth."[8] That company has a right to know the misallocation of funds.

"But, Emerson, if others are not hurt by what they don't know, it's best to be evasive. Why upset them and hurt my reputation?" Because this is another rational lie wrongly placed under the banner of being noble.

The Prideful

A wife told me that her soldier husband was asked by an acquaintance, "What rank are you now in the army?" The husband answered, "Colonel." His young son, overhearing the conversation, said, "No, you aren't, Dad, you're a captain."

One of the most common reasons people lie is to impress others. If we succeed at dazzling them, we think they will feel good about us and we will feel good about ourselves. What better reason to hedge on the truth? Everybody feels good! So let's embellish our achievements to enhance our image.

But this need not be overt. A woman told me, "My dad came over one day, and my daughter was being crazy disobedient, like her wheels came off. He asked, 'So are you putting that on Facebook?' Of course not. I have an image to project that I'm perfect, I have this great job, and I have this great daughter. I don't put the unfavorable truth out there. This doesn't fit the image I seek to project."

I refer to this as Fakebook.

I recently read about millennials who are changing the face of travel agencies. One article said, "If there's one thing millennials love more than traveling, it's bragging about the places they've traveled . . . They go for the bragging rights of being the first in their circle . . . More than 50 percent of millennials post vacation photos on social media to make friends and family jealous."[9] What a way to live. We need to post on Facebook a selfie with Mount Kilimanjaro behind us in order to brag . . . make others jealous . . . feel significant . . . like ourselves.

However, do we really wish to Photoshop our lives to ignite jealousy? The dictionary defines *Photoshop* as image editing for the purpose of distorting reality to deliberately deceive the viewer.

We must ask ourselves individually, *When I communicate what I know is untrue but favorable about myself, am I so hollow and insecure that I let my hubris compel me to write a fiction?*

The Expedient

Mark Twain said, "I would rather tell seven lies than make one explanation."[10] Because when it gets right down to it, the truth can be time consuming and tough. Truth slows things down. The truth is a hassle. But a lie gets us out of the jam. A lie is convenient. Lying is conducive to the moment. It is expedient. Why not twist the truth when I have a demanding timeline?

If I lied on FundMe.com about a business start-up to build water wells in Africa, knowing that most of the money would go in my pocket for my salary, why come clean on this when it will cause me nothing but time and trouble? It is easier to stay silent and get on with life. However, even Twain countered his advice about lying with, "The glory which is built upon a lie soon becomes a most unpleasant encumbrance. How easy it is to make people believe a lie, and how hard it is to undo that work again!"[11] What seems to be the expedient thing to do up front, that is, to lie, proves to be the costliest later in life. Ask Lance Armstrong about the heavy costs later in his life. He could not undo what he had done. Early on, his lying to the press seemed so easy and natural. I wonder if he thought, *It is so easy to make people believe a lie*. He fooled me for years. I trusted his testimony, as did millions.

By the way, why is it easier, and so quick, to lie to people? Often it is harder for the listener to detect the lie than for the liar to speak the lie. The liar takes advantage of the other's trust. The liar says to himself, "They are bound by their moral code of being a trusting person, but I have no moral code about being trustworthy and truthful. They must give me the benefit of the doubt since I am deemed innocent until proven guilty." But do we really want to live a lie even when lying is so expedient? Do we want to manipulate people's trust?

The Emotional

Emotions are wonderful but not always, not when they trump the facts.

I have frequently written pieces on our Love and Respect Facebook page, with more than two million in the feed, on a wife's need to show respect to her husband. This controversial idea is based on Ephesians 5:33 and 1 Peter 3:1–2, where wives learn of God's command to put on a respectful demeanor. As counterintuitive as it feels to a wife, it greatly influences a husband because it motivates him to be loving. However, on reading my post, certain women new to our Love and Respect Facebook page inevitably blast away in the comment section. They jump on the article as proof that my position is to always blame the woman. Because these women are new to our Love and Respect Facebook page and message, they do not check out earlier posts in which I challenge the husbands to love their wives unconditionally based on Ephesians 5:33 and Hosea 3:2. In most everything I write, I have a teeter-totter approach, going back and forth. Had these women looked at the earlier writings, they would have whistled a different tune. Instead, they judged me as imbalanced and unfair. They let their fears and feelings, probably based on their negative experiences with men, govern their words. They wrongly presume about my editorial stance. I am not saying they are irrational, but they clearly get emotional. I do not say this to put them down but to highlight their feeling-orientation as opposed to their factual-orientation.

I feel bad for those who let their feelings dictate their scathing rebukes. This is a habit in their lives, and they need to wake up. They jump the gun before they do their homework. Benjamin Franklin stated, "Presumption first blinds a Man, then sets him a running."[12]

The Bible offers the wisest of insight. Proverbs 18:13 states, "He who gives an answer before he hears, it is folly and shame to him."

Just because a woman reads our Facebook page and feels something is true about our bias against women does not make it true in fact. Feelings can be real but fickle. That's why when we make assertions without facts to back our claims, we face the prospect of looking foolish and feeling ashamed. Every effective communicator must ask first: Is it true in fact? When we speak based on facts, not on our feelings alone, we temper and restrict our comments before hitting send. I am not saying the feelings are always wrong, just that good communicators confirm their feelings with the facts. The presumption can be accurate, but the feelings first need validation.

We need to heed the advice of Sgt. Joe Friday in the 1950s TV series *Dragnet*. Though he never actually said the line on the program, he has become the legendary figure who declared and demanded, "Just the facts, ma'am."

The Inattentive

When one believes the statement to be true though the statement is false, is one a liar? No, but it is still a lie. Something doesn't become true because I believe it to be true. A lie is an untruthful statement even when the communicator believes it to be true.

Perhaps in many cases we didn't know it was untrue. No harm, no foul. Even so, an honest error in judgment does not make it okay, especially when we repeatedly make such mistakes. The real point here is to the lazy and neglectful individuals who keep making mistakes and claim they did not know the truth. They may be innocent, but one becomes guilty of carelessness and inattentiveness. We must aggressively get our facts straight to avoid a routine of "honest" mistakes.

Ignorance can create severe consequences. A medical doctor can honestly misdiagnose a condition that ends up costing a person thousands of dollars on medication, or his very life. Proverbs 14:12 states, "There is a way which seems right to a man, but its end is the way of death." Though there is no intent to deceive, sincerity doesn't prevent death. Though there is no ill will, one still needs to be forgiven for the misinformation.

Our hearts can be in the right place as we clearly communicate what we feel to be true. But that doesn't make it right any more than hitting and killing a pedestrian is to be overlooked because there was no malice or forethought. A person still died. Being inattentive is no excuse just because we have no malice.

Years ago two girls were in a car crash. One died; the other was in a coma and not recognizable. The authorities mixed their identities, and the parents of the girl in the coma were informed their daughter died. This mom and dad mourned the loss of their daughter with unspeakable grieving. However, after her funeral it was discovered that she had not died and was actually the girl in the coma. The other parents had to face the tragedy that their daughter, who they thought was alive, was deceased. Even though the authorities were kind and empathetic right after the crash, they got it wrong. Though they relayed what they deemed to be the correct information about the conditions of these two girls, it was untrue.[13]

These examples are life-and-death situations. On a

lesser scale, the good news is that most mistaken communicators can move forward by correcting the mistake. Dale Carnegie said, "There is a certain degree of satisfaction in having the courage to admit one's errors. It not only clears the air of guilt and defensiveness, but often helps solve the problem created by the error."[14] Most people are forgiving as they observe us humbly learn from our errors.

The Flatterer

Being a person who communicates what is true frequently demands tact, and at times it can feel like sidestepping land mines. It takes work to be both truthful and tactful. Some say, "I *want* to be discreet, but truth demands sincere thoughtfulness, and I am not interested in developing that skill. Telling the other person what they want to hear instead of telling them what they need to hear is the route I prefer to take with people looking for my affirmation."

This is smooth talk and disingenuous praise. This is clever lying, not tact. It is insincere. It is tickling another's ears. In many organizations some workers learn quickly to tell the boss what he wants to hear. He feels good, and they experience job security. But withholding bad news, which the boss needs to hear, doesn't make that bad news better with age and silence, as my son-in-law, Matt Reed, once shared with me.

On some occasions being truthful, tactful, and sincere is tough. What is a husband to say when his wife asks, "Does this red dress make me look fat?" A good-hearted husband longs to be truthful without being hurtful, but that isn't an easy rope to walk. Most men feel totally trapped by this question because they have learned, perhaps the hard way, that saying nothing or saying "I don't know" means "You look fat." How can he be sincere and truthful yet affirming?

What if he sincerely and tactfully says, "Well, I do like the red dress but enjoy the black dress more," to which she retorts, "So you don't like the red dress because you think I look fat? You think I am unattractive."?

What if the husband were to sincerely and tactfully say, "In the red dress you look less becoming, but I love you no matter what. You should wear whichever you prefer, though I prefer the black dress. But again, I love you in both dresses."? Elizabeth Evans Bergeron posted on the Love and Respect Facebook page about a similar situation and recommended saying, **Honey, this blue dress is more flattering of your beautiful curves. Maybe I can help you out of it later.**

Some lying only appears sincere and tactful. Telling a person what he or she wants to hear may feel like tact but not if it is a bold-faced lie. One wonders about the parents of some untalented adult children who audition for the television talent shows like *The Voice*. One of the parents should have humbly spoken the truth! "Child, God has given you talent but not as a singer."

At the same time, it is tactless and tasteless to sincerely blurt out what is true if it is received as cruel and cold-hearted. We refer to some medical doctors as lacking bedside manners. They matter-of-factly state, as they read from the chart, "Unfortunately, there is no cure. This is terminal. You have six months to live. Any questions before I leave?" Such truth without tact is heartless, though quite sincere.

The consolation is that when we work hard at being sincere, honest, and compassionate, most will receive our communication, even if it doesn't come out perfectly. They may not like what we say, but they will trust our humble, loving hearts.

When people say, "Flattery will get you everywhere," they say it tongue-in-cheek.

The Self-Deluded

Most of us have heard about an alcoholic who runs afoul of the law with DUIs, has been confronted numerous times about his binges, has lost several jobs, and often awakens in vomit. But ask him, "Are you an alcoholic?" and he'll sincerely deny that he is. He has suppressed the truth about the amount of liquor he consumes week after week (Rom. 1:18). He has convinced himself he has no problem. He can quit anytime, he tells himself.

Fyodor Dostoyevsky, in *The Brothers Karamazov*, challenges us on this front. "Above all, don't lie to yourself. The man who lies to himself and listens to his own lie comes to a point that he cannot distinguish the truth within him, or around him, and so loses all respect for himself and for others. And having no respect he ceases to love."[15]

How many of us lie to ourselves? Recently I talked with a person who finally recognized two major character flaws in himself. In discussing why it took him twenty years to see these, he said, "I did not see them as wrong because I convinced myself they were okay. I lied to myself." Of course, these two lies nearly destroyed his family. We can lull ourselves into thinking we have done no wrong. We are like the adulterer who insists, "I have done no wrong" (Prov. 30:20). Or like the son who declares, "It is not a transgression" (Prov. 28:24). Self-delusion is real.

How does this relate to thinking before hitting send? Maybe the deepest clue into why we lie to others in our communications is that we first lie to ourselves. We create *rational lies* and from these we *rationalize* that what we communicate to others is justified. This is why William Shakespeare penned, "This above all: to thine own self be true, And it must follow, as the night the day, Thou canst not then be false to any man."[16]

The Chameleon

Lauren Zander, in her article "The Truth About People-Pleasers," wrote, "You're a social chameleon on the next level—you can see from anybody's point of view, you play along with the conversation, attitudes and general disposition of whoever you are with, rather than locating your own true point of view. You don't know what you really think, and neither do they."[17]

In order to make others happy, as people pleasers are prone to do, the chameleon appears sincere in telling people what they want to hear. But the motive is to fit in at the expense of truth. This is not an accommodation in the gray areas but a compromise on black-and-white matters. For example, you are conservative with conservatives on Monday night (i.e., pro-life) and liberal with liberals on Tuesday night (i.e., pro-choice). In longing to make everyone like you, everyone eventually sees you as someone who lacks core convictions, not to suggest integrity.

The chameleon changes colors to blend in. A chameleon rationalizes as any people pleaser does. "I don't like tension and conflict." But the tactic is deception. A wife says, "I lie not to cover up bad things but to keep peace in the family unit. If I tell my husband that I bought new clothes for the kids, he'll explode. It is easier to deceive him for the sake of tranquility." She changes colors to fit in with the image she knows her husband expects her to project even though she knows it is not in accordance with the facts about what she has done.

K. W. Stout, in "Confessions of a Former People Pleaser (and Why You Should Stop Being One)," wrote, "Honesty makes life so much better. It's only hard at first, because you're so comfortable with telling little fibs and putting on an act . . . The more and more I've become brutally honest, the better my life has been. . . . Being honest with your words and actions makes life so much easier!"[18]

Before you hit send, ask yourself: *Am I a people pleaser who—unfortunately—is about to deceive others by changing colors?*

The Entrapped

As a bird following bread crumbs, some of us are lured into making a promise to guard another's lie. Sometimes other people tell us of their wrongdoings, and then they shift the focus to us. "You must not tell your spouse, boss, mother, friend, the attorney general, or anyone what I just told you about what I did wrong and my cover-up." If we swear to such secrecy about their lies, that information puts us in a position to withhold truth from others who have a right to know this truth. We are facilitating a lie.

Not only are we complicit, we are entrapped. We feel bound by an oath, like we would be doing something sacrilegious if we refuse to stay silent on their wrongdoings. How sad that we let our integrity to keep a promise (which others believe in) cause us to promise to keep secret another person's lack of integrity! Talk about ironic! They use our virtue to hide their vices. They expect us to be true to our word while they are untrue to their word. This is unscrupulous control. We end up committing treason against the truth. We must resist being subjected to this kind of coercion. People have no right to get us to swear to secrecy regarding their deceptions. For this reason we must guard against succumbing to their ability to guilt-trip us as betrayers after we refuse to keep their lies a secret. They may quickly blame us as the bad person in all of this!

As a clergyman, if a church member of mine confessed to me, for example, "I am committing adultery with my secretary, but I do not want you to tell my wife when you meet with the two of us about our marriage," I would reply, "No, I won't agree to those terms. I would be participating in your pretense, and I don't have the liberty in my heart to do that. I won't sit with your wife long term and keep from her what she has a right to know. I would sit there feeling like a liar. Instead, I expect you to tell her." If the person acted offended and tried to guilt-trip me, I would reply, "Look, the problem here is your adultery and deception. I am not the cause of your problem but am here to help you solve this problem. I care about you, your marriage, and family. I am for you. But I cannot knowingly mislead your wife."

Each of us must tread wisely and avoid keeping secret a lie that this person intends to keep telling. Whether he is doing so through social media or other ways, we must not join in with his trickery. A false narrative is a false narrative, and because we did not create the lie, but only echoed what another claimed, does not mean we get a free pass in the eyes of others.

The Protector

In the Bible, Rahab the harlot hid the spies from the king and received honor and praise from God (Josh. 2; Heb. 11:31). There is some virtue in protecting others from those who intend to harm them. However, the protective lie is rarely a noble thing even if it feels like the right thing to do.

Lisa lies to protect a work associate. "Kelli is out sick today. I talked to her. Saturday, I am taking her to the doctor." But Kelli is with her boyfriend to resolve a big fight they had the night before, so she told Lisa to cover up for her. Lisa goes along with the cover-up because she decides that lying is the better way to proceed since it helps Kelli with her relationship and protects her job. In some odd way, Lisa feels responsible to cover up for her friend instead of coming up with a plan to enable Kelli to take a vacation day or resolve the conflict after work, as other couples do.

What's the big deal? Management consists of human beings. Kelli and Lisa are lying to other human beings. Furthermore, if Lisa became the manager and Kelli lied to her about Barbara being sick, Lisa would not see Kelli as acting responsibly to protect Barbara. She'd say, "Look, get someone to cover for Barbara, but don't cover up for Barbara." We are back to the Golden Rule of true communication.

Why does this kind of thing happen in the workplace (and even among family members) more often than we imagine? There is a slight shift from "I have you covered as my friend" to "I will cover up for you as my friend." There is a difference! Then, of course, it becomes a quid pro quo situation. "You owe me." Eventually, the other covers up, and now they've formed an alliance. Oddly, both feel duty bound as responsible friends to lie for each other.

Do you find yourself advancing a narrative that is untrue so another person (or company, or political group, or whoever) does not get in trouble? Has he or she returned the favor? Rarely does this kind of thing work out. When layoffs came, Lisa and Kelli were the first to be let go. Word got out that they were not trustworthy.

And here is something else to think about. How do you know this person or group for whom you lie will never lie to you? By way of analogy, I always find it fascinating that people who have an affair and leave their spouses are in shock when the person with whom they had an affair has another affair behind their backs. I want to ask, "What did you expect? When the affair wasn't wrong with you, why should it be wrong against you?" The same holds true in companies where the workers receive honor from manage-ment for covering up the false claims about products and services. Should these workers be surprised when later management cheats them on their wages and benefits?

Bottom line, the best friendships and alliances are built on truthfulness. People who decide to tell the truth almost always find a legal and moral way to protect the interests of another, like Lisa saying to Kelli, "Let's have you take a vacation day, and I'll cover for you by working late for you tonight at work. The boss has signed off on this." It may be inconvenient and costly, but it is an hon-est plan of action. Cover-ups may feel noble as a way of protecting another's agenda, but at the end of the day, it is just lying, and lying is not the best policy.

The Chronic

As all parents eventually learn, children are moral and spiritual beings who know truth from a lie. Infants mislead their parents with their fake cries, toddlers learn to lie by breaking established rules and feigning ignorance, and the average five-year-old becomes quite skilled at successfully lying to others.

Does this sound too severe? I predict that most of us recall an early point in our lives when we made a decision to lie or not lie as a way of dealing with problems. My observation is that chronic liars began in preschool. Those who are not chronic liars made a decision to stop the tendency to lie at that same time period.

Unfortunately, Joe never made that decision when he was young.

Today Joe has a quiver full of lies that he uses. He texts a family member to say he's running late due to traffic and because his neighbor dropped in to ask his opinion on an electrical problem, which also put him behind. Neither of these is true, but lies fuel Joe's lifestyle. At work, when writing an e-mail about some issue, if he can, to get through the problem, he pulls a lie from his quiver: **Hey, I didn't see that e-mail about the Clifford account. I will need to get back to you after I find it. Sorry, I will need another day on this.** Of course, that's a lie. He saw the e-mail. When receiving a voice message at home from his boss about showing up for work on Saturday morning, he later tells the boss he never received that call. He thinks one of his kids hit "delete all" on the voice messages on their home phone. Joe always thinks about how to lie since, to Joe, other things he is doing are more important. This is ingrained from childhood. It is a default reaction. It seems second nature.

Some argue that a chronic liar like Joe will never change. However, I am more hopeful for such a person. Like any addictive behavior, a person can bring it under control. Certainly the Bible gives us that hope. Peter wrote, "Therefore, putting aside . . . all deceit . . ." (1 Peter 2:1). It is possible and expected. The incentive for Joe to change his chronic lying is that it is unlikely he will succeed in life when those who promote and reward say to one another, "Joe really isn't truthful or trustworthy."

The Copycat

We tell our kids, "Just because others take drugs doesn't mean that you can take drugs. Because others drive recklessly doesn't mean you can. We are not copycats in this family. We don't go along with the crowd."

Just because everybody lies at one time or another in childhood or adulthood does not make this a universal principle and therefore an okay thing to do. We must not proclaim this as an inevitable law of nature (though it would be appropriate to assert it is part of sinful human nature).

When family and friends lie, we must resist the idea that we have no other choice but to go along with it. We have a choice, albeit a tough one. One article reported, "Our results indicate that a person's lying tendencies can be predicted by the lying tendencies of his or her friends and family members."[19] The company we keep can influence us to lie unless we take steps to resist that influence. We must say no to lying; otherwise, our family and friends can pull us into that swamp. That is why the Bible warns, "Do not be deceived: 'Bad company corrupts good morals'" (1 Cor. 15:33).

When an adult sibling tweets a lie about the supposed horrible treatment by a local business, will we be a puppet on a string and echo him in a tweet for no other reason than he's our brother? Will we let him corrupt our morals? Or, when our work associate lies to a customer, will we stand behind him and support his lie lest we be excluded from the in-crowd from work that meets daily for lunch? Copycats believe they have little say but that's not so. Each of us can be truth-tellers who stand strong and stay true to our convictions and conscience. We need not throw away our moral compass, even though we are never again invited to lunch.

Unless wicked men have kidnapped Grandma and are

holding her hostage until we lie, steal, and cheat to get the ransom money, all our moments are under our control and reflect our convictions. It is inaccurate to say, "I don't want to lie, but the people around me lie so I must play according to the game plan." We are not helpless and hopeless. Copycatting is a decision we make. This is not monkey see, monkey do. We are spiritual beings made in the image of God who control our own moral destinies.

The Perpetuator

One person wrote to me, explaining, "Once in a custody battle between my guardians for me, I said one had not fed me. I was four or so, but I figured it was wrong. I really didn't mean it to go so far." Indeed, a lie can go far fast, and we have to stay out in front of it, and this can begin when we're in preschool.

Another wrote what it is like to perpetually lie. "Juggling 3 different girls at the same time who don't know about each other. Having to come up with excuses why you can't spend time with one of them because you booked it with the other one. Trying to remember which excuse you made to which girl, and then trying to come up with stories that happened at the fake event. It's hard work."[20] People who live carnal, selfish lives prove how stupid and unloving it is to lie.

One lie feeds on another lie like a food chain. The

first small lie becomes food for a slightly larger lie, which in turn feeds a bigger lie. You get the picture. Such lying snowballs. We lie about the lie, and then lie about the lie about the lie. It is endless and expansive! Lies can grow exponentially like a spreading cancer without a cure. One lives each day having to be ready to lie about the plethora of lies. Truly, it is a web of lies. It is demanding and draining to stay out in front of the lie. Many have finally said, "I am done with lying. It isn't worth it. I am exhausted." We who are perpetuating lies need to stop. We must not wait until death when others read on our tombstones: "Finally, He No Longer Lies Where He Lies!"

In our last chapter we address the role of confession. Some of us need to get this monkey off our backs. We cannot outrun an avalanche. It will catch up to us. When caught in all our lies and forced to confess, who will believe we are authentic? But taking the initiative on our own sends the message of sincerity and remorse. Most people forgive those who want to stop perpetuating falsehoods. And, when we come clean, we feel clean!

The Ashamed

Lies are almost always related to what we have done wrong ethically, legally, or morally. We lie to cover up our past wrongdoings. We lie to cover up our future wrong-doings. We lie about our present wrongdoings.

For most of us, when we violate what is legal or moral, we feel shame. At that point we are at a crossroads. Will we confess, or will we conceal?

Several years ago my wife, Sarah, was caught speeding. As the officer approached the car, Sarah exclaimed, "I am guilty. I deserve a ticket. Please give me a ticket. I think I was going like thirty miles over." Stunned, the officer said, "Lady, in all my years as a policeman, no one has ever said, 'Give me a ticket.' Ma'am, go on your way. Have a good day." Sarah then argued with him because she honestly deserved a ticket and wasn't afraid of the truth or the cost, as problematic as that might be. Why did Sarah respond this way? She doesn't lie when she is ashamed of wrongdoing. In the face of shame, she tells the truth to come clean. Pretty simple.

"But, Emerson, what if telling the truth is costly, far more than a speeding ticket?" Telling the truth may cost us everything, as it does with an embezzler confessing his crime and going to prison. Or a husband confessing his adultery and his wife divorcing him and taking the kids to another state. However, it isn't the truth that is costing us everything; it is our wrongdoing. Truth is not the enemy.

I wish I could say something softer to those who have done serious crime, but I cannot. I can say that believers in Christ who come clean experience the peace of Christ, a clear conscience, meaningful meditations in Scripture, renewed power in prayer, joy in worship at church, and a fruitful ministry among sinners. None of these things were happening earlier due to the hidden sin and shame. Many have told me, "It is a trade-off but well worth it." I have observed husbands confess their adultery and be happier at that moment than they have been for months, even though their world is falling apart. Coming out from under shame is a very good thing.

Have we lied in an e-mail, a staff meeting, over the phone, in a report, about a product or service? Wherever we have lied, we cannot remove shame by lying about the lie. That never, ever works. Only the truth removes the shame. Yes, the truth reveals the guilt, but the honest confession removes the shame. When we are honest about our dishonesty, the shame lifts. We are now doing what is right and good.

The Oath-Maker

We have all been around people who exclaim, "Honest to God, I am telling you the truth. I swear to God." In effect, they take the Lord's name in vain.

They aren't "honest to God." They are dishonest to God, and others. They are lying under their own oath, doing so to manipulate others into believing the lie is not a lie. Such people lack confidence in the truth of their own words (because they aren't telling the truth), so they use God as the trump card to win over the other person. They want the other to conclude, "Anyone who swears to God must be honest to God, and must be honest with me. I will buy what they sell."

Do liars make oaths and swear to God? Perhaps more than most! "A liar," wrote Pierre Corneille, "is always lavish of oaths."[21] And as Vittorio Alfieri said, "Liars are always most disposed to swear."[22]

Jesus said, "Make no oath . . . by heaven, for it is the throne of God" (Matt. 5:34). He continued, "But let your statement be, 'Yes, yes' or 'No, no'; anything beyond these is of evil" (v. 37).

Before we hit send, let's think: Am I about to make an oath by swearing to God about something I know isn't true? Is that what I should do? Would Jesus say to me, "What you are about to communicate is wrong. Though it is easy enough for you to swear, bringing God into the conversation, this is actually evil in My eyes"?

The Brainy

Though today we may get by with a lie, next month we must recall the lies and the truth as we spoke them. This is hard and time-consuming work. "What did I say in September about why I could not get the report done by January 15? Where is that doggone e-mail that reminds me of what I said?!" To lie effectively, we must remember both narratives.

Each of us must weigh his or her intelligence. Do we have a photographic memory so that we can recall all lies and all truths? Or do we lack that kind of genius and know we'll end up forgetting what we said? It may not be the most noble of reasons, but some of us say, "I refuse to lie because I am not that smart." On the other hand, some of us stupidly give way to lies because we observe politicians and business leaders lying and getting away with it. "If they can, I can." Again, though, they are very smart people who believe they can get away with it and have made the decision that their ends justify their deceptive means. They don't feel uncomfortable with being someone other than "Honest Abe." Of course, I happen to believe that no one ever gets away with a lie. It is only a matter of time on earth or in heaven. We read in 1 Timothy 5:24, "The sins of some people are obvious, going ahead of them to judgment. The sins of others follow them there" (GW).

This is why we must decide what professions we wish to enter and what types of persons we will become within those professions. Most of us would agree with Ralph Waldo Emerson: "Character is higher than intellect."[23]

Whether or not we are brainy, we are wise enough not to lie. In the end, it isn't worth it, and the smart people figure this out!

The Wordsmith

A pastor I know left his first pastorate after only a year, but he then spent more than forty years at his next church. When I asked him about the extreme opposites in tenure, he said it was due to the bullfrog illustration.

"Bullfrogs in a pond have the ability to echo, which gives the impression that scores of bullfrogs reside in the pond when actually there may be just one or two. In my first pastorate, a person said to me, 'Everybody is saying they don't like what you do as a pastor.' At the time, I didn't know he was a bullfrog. He gave me the impression that the majority of the congregation disliked me. I left the church. His comments empowered him, and it worked.

"In the second church a person told me the bullfrog story, so when complaints arose, I would ask, 'Who feels this way?' They wouldn't name anybody, so I decided to disbelieve them. I did not want to discount their concerns, but I refused to make a major decision based on their individual croakings. When they claimed 'everyone,' they were making a misleading comment. Maybe 'everyone' in their clique felt as they felt, but not 'everyone' in the church."

I once heard that a report was given about a battle in Vietnam. The American military told the press that our casualties were light. What they meant was that the soldiers were all under 160 pounds. Maybe that example of wordsmithing is a bit more extreme than what we are guilty of, but don't we still wordsmith ourselves in ways that are ambiguous at best and intentionally misleading at worst? Have you ever said any of the following? If so, what would have been your answer had you been asked the follow-up question?

- "Everybody feels this way."
  Who?
- "Experience has proven . . ."
  The experience of whom?
- "There is a growing body of evidence . . ."
  Please show it to me.
- "This is award winning."
  Who gave the award and why?
- "Our product is regarded as the best."
  Based on what test and criteria?
- "Research reveals . . ."
  Who did the study, and were there opposing studies?[24]

The intent behind wordsmithing is not always bad. People can have compassion and goodwill. Don't we soften a little when we learn the company didn't "fire" people but rather they "downsized"? Do we not prefer the government use the term "job seekers" rather than "unemployed"? And don't the police use "physical persuasion," not "violence"?

None of these expressions are inherently bad, but they do serve to remind us that we can cross a line into misleading statements. Using discretion is one thing, deception another.

The Self-Amuser

"On the whole, lying is a cheerful affair," wrote Isabel Fonseca. "Embellishments are intended to give pleasure. People long to tell you what they imagine you want to hear. They want to amuse you; they want to amuse themselves; they want to show you a good time. This is beyond hospitality. This is art."[25] Think about it. Why do some people exaggerate? They wish to entertain. In many social settings, we give grace to the storyteller who embellishes the funny episode.

However, there is someone other than the entertainer. There are those who find delight in misleading others. As tough as this is for me to say, some people enter politics because they derive personal fulfillment from the "gotcha" approach to issues. It isn't about what is true but about the political chess game. The key is to put a better spin on a matter than the other candidate and to put the opposition in checkmate. It took me a while to figure this out because I found myself exhausted by the thought of being in this fray day after day. Then one day it hit me: "They like this polemical game. This amuses them more than I imagine. It is a contest that invigorates them." Furthermore, in this environment they do not suffer the liability for slander and lies. The courts give them a pass in politics. They can pull a statement their opponent said in passing and broadcast that but remove the follow-up comment that said, "Having said that, let me explain why that might not be true." Rightly representing is not the name of the game. Winning is the name of the game. Thus, after a TV interview they high-five it with their party peers when their spin of misleading comments proves persuasive.

Am I off base? Why do we often hear the statement, "You can fool all the people some of the time, and some of the people all the time, but you cannot fool all the people all the time"? The person quoting this comment knows that there are some people involved in trying to trick the masses, though ultimately they cannot pull it off. Oddly, a few do it for the challenge and fun of it. They derive a weird sense of delight in trying to fool large numbers of people on a regular basis. An expression currently used is "fake news." There are any number of reasons people create fake news, but some do it for one reason: it is a game to see if they can get away with it.

Before we hit send we need to ask: Is this about what I can get away with for self-amusing purposes?

Why Should We Communicate
What Is True?

Our trustworthiness rests on our truthfulness. When Teddy Roosevelt was a cattle rancher, he and a new cowboy were riding across a section of his land when they came across a maverick, an unbranded yearling from a neighboring ranch. It had wandered onto Teddy's land, and he instructed the cowboy to brand it with his neighbor's brand, as was the custom. Roosevelt recounted that the man replied, "'All right, Boss; I know my business.' 'Hold on a minute,' I said; 'you are putting on my brand.' He said, 'I always put on the Boss's brand.' And then I said, 'Oh! all right; go back and get your time.' He said, 'What's that for?' And I said, 'My friend, if you will steal for me, you will steal from me.'"[26]

Roosevelt had learned a sad but true reality. One who steals for you is a thief, and thieves will steal from you when the occasion enables it.

The same holds true with the person who lies. The one who lies for you will lie to you.

Do we lie at work? Once others at our place of employment suspect us of being untruthful, the whispering behind our backs begins. When we compromise the truth, our credibility sinks speedily. People can't stand liars. Actually, they fear the liar could lie about them or lie to them. Lying feels dark to people. Satan himself is referred to as a liar.

For certain, once we are viewed as one who lies, will we be believed when telling the truth? Unlikely. If we wish to be trustworthy, we must be truthful. As Michael Josephson said, "Honesty doesn't always pay, but dishonesty always costs."[27]

Truth helps people, so we must have the courage to speak it. Because I pastored in a college town, many young couples requested that I do their weddings. Before I would agree, they needed to participate in our church's six-week premarital course, which included testing. The leadership of the church made this mandatory, making it clear that if any red flags appeared, they reserved the right to say no to doing the ceremony on our premises. The couples knew this ahead of time. Every so often we had to say no. It was never easy. The bride and groom were hurt. However, I recall one set of parents profusely thanking us for refusing to do the wedding since they saw red flags all over the place but felt they could not say anything. They were forever grateful that we cared enough to confront.

Telling the truth based on our premarital assessment tools was not joyful, but we knew this was the right thing to do. Our motives were pure. Our counseling was free. We desired to help these couples succeed in their marriages. We knew the best predictor of future behavior was past behavior, and because these couples had serious behavioral issues from the past, there was no reason to believe anything would change unless they changed first. We needed to humbly but candidly tell them the truth. This took courage.

Though many couples were unhappy with our assessments, there were others we counseled to postpone their marriages until these past issues were addressed who humbly responded, "Please tell us what we need to do." More than three decades later some of these couples, who later married, are some of our best friends. The truth helped them immeasurably.

We must not let fear keep us from telling the truth. Plato said, "I shall assume that your silence gives consent."[28]

A most significant point of this book is this: If what we think is true, kind, necessary, and clear, we need to have the courage to hit send. This isn't about refraining from speaking; this is about speaking. Please hear me. Hit send!

God never lies, and He calls us to imitate Him. Many of us are aware of certain Bible verses, such as, "God is not a man, that He should lie" (Num. 23:19); "It is impossible for God to lie" (Heb. 6:18); or "God, who cannot lie" (Titus 1:2). Then we read in Ephesians 5:1, "Therefore be imitators of God, as beloved children," to which most of us react, "Well, I can't be perfect. I can't be like God and never, ever lie."

But if that is so, then why does God call us to lay "aside falsehood" and "speak truth" (Eph. 4:25)? He does not favor those who love and practice lying (Rev. 22:15).

Because God loves us, He will not ignore our lying. Jesus revealed, "But I tell you that every careless word that people speak, they shall give an accounting for it in the day of judgment" (Matt. 12:36). Romans 14:12 states, "Each one of us will give an account of himself to God." Is this a fear tactic designed by biblical writers, and even Jesus, to scare people into conformity? Should this notion of a judgment be rejected since some create a caricature of God as a cosmic Killjoy ready to pounce on us for fibbing? Each of us must decide what he or she believes. For me, I take seriously what Jesus said. I would prefer not to believe it, but I must. I have chosen to trust Christ both for His promises and His warnings.

"But, Emerson, God will forgive us of all sins, including our lies. Christ died on the cross to pay the penalty for all of my sins, including my lies." Yes, but there are two things you and I cannot halt. One, God's loving discipline of us on earth for lying. Read Hebrews 12 about the love of God prompting His fatherly discipline of us as His children. In other words, He loves us too much to turn a deaf ear to our falsehoods. As an earthly father rebukes and corrects a son who lies, God does the same with us. Second, though eternal life is a gift based on our faith in Christ, who paid the penalty for all of our sins, God provides an add-on called "rewards." Once in heaven, which we cannot earn, there are rewards given to the forgiven! God rewards us for what we have done. These rewards are important because God says they are important. Some believers at the judgment will receive no rewards. I am supposing that the careless words to which Jesus referred (Matt. 12:36), and about which we must give account, will be a contributing factor to never receiving His rewards and can cause us to lose the rewards we had gained, according to the apostle John (2 John 1:8)! Those who live their lives in the kingdom of this world, advancing the lies of their worldly associations, will one day realize they built their houses on sand (Matt. 7:26) instead of on the words of Jesus in imitation of Him. For the true believer, this matters more than what can be gained by the lie—infinitely more.

Truth is easier to remember than the truth plus lies. As I said earlier, many of us have decided to be truth-tellers for less than noble reasons. We realize we aren't smart enough to remember both the truths and the lies, and we are bound to get caught in a lie. This is why during cross-examination the lawyer asks the same question, varied this and that way, six or eight times over a two-hour deposition. If the interrogated person is lying, he cannot keep track of all the details that he fabricated earlier.

Telling the truth is so much easier.

The story goes that in court one day the prosecuting attorney raised his voice at a boy who had spent the last twenty minutes on the witness stand and exclaimed, "Be honest, son. Your dad told you what to say in court, didn't he?" The boy replied, "Yes sir, he did." The lawyer gleefully thought he had snared the kid. "Okay, son, what did he tell you to say?" Humbly, the boy said, "He told me, 'Son, just tell the truth, and you need only say the same thing over and over when questioned.'"

I love that story. Mark Twain wrote, "If you tell the truth you don't have to remember anything."[29]

Show me a person who is a truthful communicator in e-mails, tweets, phone calls, lunch meetings, and at family gatherings and so forth, and I will show you a person who has concluded, "Lies are too wearisome and worrisome."

How Can We Respond to Others Who Communicate What Is Untrue?

Do you have a family member, friend, or coworker who hedges on the truth? Have you wondered how to approach him or her? Here are some jump-starter recommendations on what to say to someone who is untruthful around us.

- TO THE FEARFUL ("Honestly, I dread the consequences over past missteps, so I cover them up."), say,

    "I need you to be courageous no matter the consequences. When fear causes you to withhold truth, I need you to bravely declare, 'I can handle the truth!'"

- TO THE SELFISH ("What can I say? Lying works to my advantage, advancing my agenda."), say,

    "I need mutual respect here. When you lie to serve yourself, I feel used and useless as a human being. I matter, too, and must live with myself, as well as with you."

- TO THE EVASIVE ("If others don't know what I did wrong, there'll be fewer problems all around."), say,

    "I need your total transparency. When you evade my questions, I'm suspicious. I suspect a cover-up when you avoid me, saying, 'I don't know' or pleading the fifth."

- TO THE PRIDEFUL ("I need to look better than I am so others will feel good about me and like me."), say,

    "I need you to be you. You may not like who you are, but I do. However, I cannot have a relationship with someone who isn't humbly honest about who they are."

- TO THE EXPEDIENT ("I lie since it is quicker and easier for me at the moment."), say,

  "I need you to resist the convenience of lying. Today you may get by with a lie, but next month you must remember it exactly to do damage control. That's long, hard work."

- TO THE EMOTIONAL ("If it feels true, I say it. I don't need all the facts when I feel I'm right."), say,

  "I need you to stop making assumptions based only on feelings. Your feelings are real, but that does not necessarily make them right. You need facts to back your feelings."

- TO THE INATTENTIVE ("I didn't know that what I said was inaccurate; everyone makes mistakes."), say,

  "I need your integrity but also accuracy. Your heart is in the right place. But I need you to be more careful about making fewer slipups; that extra effort will pay off."

- TO THE FLATTERER ("I want to be truthful plus tactful, but insincere praise works better for me."), say,

  "I need your affirmation. I really do. But I do not need your false flattery. Your lie discredits you and hurts me. I need honesty spoken lovingly and respectfully."

- TO THE SELF-DELUDED ("Some claim I lie to

myself. But that's a lie. I'm 100 percent honest with myself."), say,

"I need you to stop believing what is false is true and what is true is false. Facing the facts is hard. None of us enjoys seeing our shortcomings, but it is necessary for success."

- TO THE CHAMELEON ("To duck conflict, I bend my beliefs to fit my audience, which pleases them."), say,

"I need you to see how you lose your identity by blending in like a chameleon with every belief. Not only does this lessen your credibility, but you have no core convictions. True?"

- TO THE ENTRAPPED ("It's not my fault. I was lured into swearing secrecy and facilitated a lie."), say,

"Don't let your integrity cause you to promise to keep secret another's lack of integrity! What a contradiction! They are taking advantage of you. This is a losing game for you."

- TO THE PROTECTOR ("I feel responsible to protect another's interests even if I have to lie to do so."), say,

"I need you to be protective. But don't protect another by lying. You're not doing anyone a favor by lying to them. That's not a virtue; it's enablement."

- TO THE CHRONIC ("I've always lied even when the truth was better. Something comes over me."), say,

"I agree that you lie when you don't need to.

Lying seems ingrained to you. What will motivate you to change? Let's think it through together and come up with a different plan."

- TO THE COPYCAT ("I'm not really interested in lying, but everybody else lies, so I do too."), say,

  "Remember your mother's advice: 'If someone jumps off a cliff, don't you jump off a cliff'? This is not about other people. This is about you. You need not mimic others and thereby compromise your integrity. Don't shift the responsibility off of yourself."

- TO THE PERPETUATOR ("I lie to stay out ahead of other lies I have told; sadly, lies beget lies."), say,

  "I need you to tell the truth up front. Then you won't have to lie about lying. You'll be so much happier when you don't have to worry about keeping up with what you've said."

- TO THE ASHAMED ("I'm a bit humiliated over the bad stuff I've done, so I lie to appear good."), say,

  "You can lie about your immorality and appear moral. But you can't feel moral by your lying. You can't remove shame with a lie. Actually, you increase the sense of shame."

- TO THE OATH-MAKER ("I admit, when hedging, I swear to God so others believe what I'm saying."), say,

  "I need you to see that even though you say, 'Honest to God,' you haven't been. You lie by using the phrase 'honest to God.' You swear by heaven to lie. That's just a very bad idea."

- TO THE BRAINY ("I'm smart, retaining both the lies and truth. It's easy to get away with lying."), say,

    "Only a pure genius can recall all lies and all truths. You and I will forget. And even if you're a genius who can remember it all, you're still lying. Telling the truth is so much smarter."

- TO THE WORDSMITH ("I find it easy and fun to twist words, using double meanings that mislead."), say,

    "You're great with words, but I need you to figure out why you try to mislead others with them. You have plenty to be proud of without exaggerating and tricking people with double meanings."

- TO THE SELF-AMUSER ("Frankly, I view tricking others as an exciting and entertaining game."), say,

    "Lying just to see if you can get away with it is a cruel game. Why do you think you do that? Are you bored? Is there some group you're trying to impress with how smart you are in fooling others?"

In Conclusion

If our communication is not true, what good is it to go on speaking about kind, necessary, and clear communication?

Truth is the heart of the other three components of wise communication.

But more so, lying is not restricted to the horizontal. There is a bigger and more important vertical dimension. Rationalizing the lies, minimizing their seriousness, and fantasizing about getting away with untruths is not an option for one who truly believes in God. At the end of the day and at the end of our lives, this is between God and us. Our secret lies won't escape our loving Lord's notice. Paul wrote, "God will judge the secrets of men through Christ Jesus" (Rom. 2:16). The believer realizes what Peter said to Ananias. "Why is it that you have conceived this deed in your heart? You have not lied to men but to God" (Acts 5:4).

Our communication is very important to God. As odd as this sounds, God is reading our mail, and when we are not truthful, we are not truthful with Him. It isn't that we cannot lie, but we ask, *Why would I when I love God and He loves me, and my communication is really a reflection of my communion with Him?* This is our deepest mind-set before hitting send. We have an audience of One.

If we are uncertain if something is a lie, can we pray about it? Can we bring the matter before God? In *The Adventures of Huckleberry Finn*, Mark Twain wrote, "You can't pray a lie—I found that out."[30]

One final word. Why have I focused more on untrue communication than on true communication? We tend to learn better when something is stated in the negative. God knew this, so He gave us the Ten Commandments. Eight of the commandments are "Thou Shalt Not." Put it this way: I pay attention when reading "Do Not Run Around the Pool Lest You Slip, Fall, and Die." I remember it more than I would "Walk Around the Pool, Be Safe, and Live Long."

Having said that, let's be inspired by the following positives about truthful communication.

Socially, we will be

- **Trusted:** People trust us when we are predictable truth-tellers.
- **Credible:** Truthfulness on small matters makes us credible on important matters.
- **Supported:** When people trust us as truthful, they support our right to our beliefs.
- **Persuasive:** Others listen to and are persuaded by us when we always tell the truth.
- **Reputable:** We have a far more credible reputation as a truth-teller.
- **Examples:** We are the best of examples to children when we tell the truth.
- **Real:** We live life in touch with reality.

- **Trusting:** We trust others initially, which creates positive interactions up front.

Personally, we will be

- **Innocent:** Our habitual honesty gives us a clear conscience.
- **Restful:** Always telling the truth gives us peace of mind, and we sleep well.
- **Free:** We live free of exposure since there is nothing to expose.
- **Healthy:** Less stress and better health comes to us as truth-tellers.
- **Self-Esteemed:** Walking in integrity enables us to feel good about ourselves.
- **Self-Advancing:** Honesty is the best policy since it best advances our long-term interests.
- **Simpler:** Over a lifetime, telling the truth makes our lives so much easier.
- **God-like:** Our truth-telling imitates God, who never lies.

CHAPTER 2

IS IT KIND?

Scriptural Meditation on Kind Speech

- Ephesians 4:15—But **speaking the truth in love**, we are to grow up in all aspects into Him who is the head, even Christ.
- 1 Corinthians 13:4—Love is **kind** . . .
- Proverbs 15:1—A **gentle answer** turns away wrath, but a harsh word stirs up anger.
- 2 Timothy 2:25—**With gentleness correcting** those who are in opposition, if perhaps God may grant them repentance leading to the knowledge of the truth.
- Colossians 4:6—**Let your speech always be with grace,**

---

as though seasoned with salt, so that you will know how you should respond to each person.

- 1 Peter 3:9—Don't pay back evil with evil. **Don't pay back unkind words with unkind words. Instead, pay back evil with kind words.** This is what you have been chosen to do. You will receive a blessing by doing this (NIrV).
- 1 Corinthians 4:13—When we are slandered, **we answer kindly** (NIV).
- Proverbs 16:21-24—The wise in heart will be called understanding, and **sweetness of speech increases persuasiveness.** Understanding is a fountain of life to one who has it, but the discipline of fools is folly. The heart of the wise instructs his mouth and adds persuasiveness to his lips. Pleasant words are a honeycomb, sweet to the soul and healing to the bones.
- Proverbs 12:25—Anxiety weighs down the heart, but **a kind word cheers it up** (NIV).
- Proverbs 15:4—**Kind words are good medicine,** but deceitful words can really hurt (CEV).
- Proverbs 19:22—What is desirable in a man is his **kindness.**
- Micah 6:8—He has told you, O man, what is good; and what does the LORD require of you but to do justice, **to love kindness,** and to walk humbly with your God?
- Ecclesiastes 10:12—Words from the mouth of a wise man are **gracious,** while the lips of a fool consume him.

- **1 Peter 3:15**—But sanctify Christ as Lord in your hearts, always being ready to make a defense to everyone who asks you to give an account for the hope that is in you, yet with **gentleness and reverence**.
- **Colossians 3:8**—But now you also, put them all aside: anger, wrath, malice, slander, and **abusive speech from your mouth**.
- **Proverbs 12:18**—There is one who **speaks rashly** like the thrusts of a sword, but the tongue of the wise brings healing.
- **Proverbs 25:15**—By forbearance a ruler may be persuaded, and a **soft tongue** breaks the bone.
- **Luke 4:22**—And all were speaking well of Him, and wondering at **the gracious words which were falling from His lips**; and they were saying, "Is this not Joseph's son?"

Is It Loving and Respectful?

People hear your words of truth, but they feel your words of kindness. In other words, they feel your love and respect. I am defining *kindness* as being a loving and respectful person.

Thumper the rabbit said, "If you can't say something nice, don't say nothing at all."[1] I prefer to say if you do not appear as a caring and honorable person when you speak, don't say anything at all, at least not yet. Words that sound unloving and disrespectful stomp on the hearts of people and discredit us.

Some believe kindness is optional, a nicety, like table manners where one must use the smaller fork with a salad and the larger fork with the main course. On my Love and Respect Facebook page someone commented, **Truth and honesty are the best thing any one must have. Kindness is just a plus.** I disagree. This is not a nice add-on. When you are truthful all day long while being unkind, hateful, and contemptuous, you are making more enemies than friends. I once heard a person say, "When I know you hate me, I cannot hear you." Our hostility and disdain close off the spirits of others to the very truth we wish them to hear.

Some feel that kindness compromises the truth. They equate kindness with giving others license to indulge their hedonistic appetites. However, kindness is not about acquiescing or agreeing with others' positions. Kindness has to do with who we are as persons. We are caring and honorable people who deliver the uncompromising truth in a loving and respectful manner. Though a kind person has a demeanor that seeks to be understanding and empathetic toward another's position, this kind person refuses to exchange the truth for a lie. Absolute truth is nonnegotiable. But truth is not advanced by being mean-spirited, hateful, and rude. Being nasty and uncharitable does not guard the truth but discredits the truth and us.

In any interaction between human beings, we must work diligently to speak in loving and respectful ways. In Ephesians 5:33, God commands a husband and wife, the most intimate of relationships, to show love and respect in their marriage. That's why we need to learn from couples who succeed in marriage. One husband wrote, "Our arguments would escalate not because of what the argument was over but because I would come across as unloving and she would come across as disrespectful. Now, we take a step back and try to understand where the other is coming from and why we are angry at each other. We have found that most of our fights are because we act in unloving or disrespectful ways, not over the little thing that triggered the fight."

I have observed that labor unions and management oftentimes fail to come to an agreement not because the proposals are unreasonable but because during the process unions felt management didn't care and management felt the unions did not respect them. When there is an undercurrent of mean-spiritedness, it subverts the trust and thus the deliberations. When it comes to negotiations, some deals can be more than fair but our rudeness sabotages the proposal.

A question for all of us to ask before communicating is, "Am I addressing the issue or attacking the person?" If the other feels attacked as a person, the negotiations will be very difficult. When attacked, we put up walls and close off our spirit. We may be present, but we are so guarded that we don't really listen.

How about you? During a conflict, do you approach another as an ally not an enemy, a friend not a foe? Do you assume he or she has goodwill and is trustworthy until you know for a fact that the person is untrustworthy and lacks goodwill?

Do you seek to remain positive and affirming while addressing the concerns on the table?

When seeking to persuade others or affect their hearts, we need to keep asking, *How can I speak what is true and necessary and clear without others feeling I am unkind? How can I differ with people without them feeling unloved and disrespected?*

The Heart of Communicating What Is Kind

I once heard a story about a Frenchman who was a believer in Jesus Christ. He lived under the Nazi regime during World War II and harbored Jews until the Germans caught him. He was brought before a German officer known as the Torturer. As this godly Frenchman entered the presence of this Nazi officer, the peace of Christ flooded his soul—a peace that passes all comprehension, as the Bible reveals. This officer observed his tranquil expression and interpreted it as snideness. Everyone else who stood in his presence manifested total fear. This soldier of the Gestapo screamed, "Get that snide look off your face! Don't you know who I am?" There was a brief pause, and the Frenchman humbly replied, "Yes, sir. I know who you are. You are known as the Torturer, and you have the power to torture me and kill me." Then, taking a step toward the officer, he kindly said, "But sir, you do not have the power to get me to hate you."

In a similar way, the heart of my communication means the other person cannot get my heart to be unkind, unloving, or disrespectful. Instead, I have made a decision about who I will be, independent of the other person. I won't blame my unkindness on someone else.

In hitting send, if I am feeling provoked by another's maddening behavior and react like a madman, I will be seen as a madman along with the other person. I get no pass because he or she started it. Even though the other person came at me first, my insane reaction reveals to others that I have a serious character flaw. My rude and mean-spirited reaction reveals me as a rude and mean-spirited person.

———

Too, we may not intend to be unkind (our hearts are in the right place), but it makes little difference when others interpret our communication as unloving and disrespectful. A person wrote to me:

> During the search process to hire someone, which I was part of, I was hurt by some nasty stuff said to me. Rather than being thick skinned and letting insults lay at the cross of Christ, I aired my hurt to a friend who lived out of state. Bad choice. I learned that e-mail is about as private as the cable news. My opinions shared in frustration were shared with no less than the entire search committee and spouses. The person in whom I confided, hoping for an understanding shoulder to lean on, betrayed that confidence. I will probably never communicate with that person again. I cannot trust this person to this day. After I apologized to the search committee for the hurt I caused by my words, I made such e-mails a thing of my past. I failed the test, and will forever remember the lessons it taught me. I am ashamed of the fact that I cracked under pressure, but I learned not to assume that distant others will keep confidences. I also learned what a small world it is electronically. I thank God that I could learn from this experience and that I can teach my children from it.

When we communicate in ways that sound unloving and disrespectful, will we blame others and circumstances for our unkind remarks? For example, as the family of six drives a half mile away from McDonald's, Dad looks in the paper bags and notices that two of the orders are missing. In disbelief, he turns the car around and heads back. As he enters the front doors and goes to the counter, he exclaims to the manager, "I can't believe your incompetency; no wonder you work here. You failed to put in the two Happy Meals we ordered. Everyone here is one french fry short of a Happy Meal." After the manager gives him what he wants, this dad walks out in a huff. He will give himself plausible reasons for his behavior since he feels offended and inconvenienced. Being an honorable man who speaks respectfully doesn't enter his mind. Being a caring individual on the heels of others being careless passes him by. To him, the extent to which he communicates "kindly" is the extent he loses power and influence; besides, he'll never see them again. His anger and autonomy assuage his guilt. But we all know he could have achieved the same objective by walking in and saying, "Hey, a mistake was made. Can you help me here?"

Here's a critical question: Did their carelessness cause him to be angry and disrespectful or reveal him to be an angry and disrespectful person? I love to remind myself that the sun hardens the clay but melts the butter. By that I mean the sun doesn't cause the clay to harden and butter to melt. The sun reveals the inner properties of each. When things heat up, it is then I reveal my true colors.

Truth be told, our unkindness comes from within. Jesus said in Mark 7:21–22, "For from within, out of the heart of men, proceed . . . slander . . ." But we think it is caused by others and that we must even the score with our rudeness. Other people do not cause us to be the way we are; they reveal our predisposition to express disgust and disparagement.

The Golden Rule of Kind Communication

Are people unkind in today's social world? Some are. One problem area is trolling. "Trolling . . . means posting inflammatory or provocative remarks on a social network or forum to trigger an emotional response, deliberately provoking other users or readers into arguing back."[2]

But none of us can stand it when people are unfriendly and mean-spirited toward us, whether online or out in the real world. We know kindness is fundamental for relationships to work well in the family, neighborhood, legislature, workplace, or wherever. We avoid unsympathetic, inconsiderate, and nasty people. For instance, we take our business elsewhere when a store owner talks to us in an uncaring and callous way.

But when pushed to the edge ourselves and feeling kindness is getting us nowhere, do we turn unpleasant, disagreeable, and uncivil? Do we compromise kindness to get what we want or to prevent losing what we have? Do we appear hostile and contemptuous? Do we intimidate? Do we bully? Do we use abusive speech? Or are we committed to speaking lovingly and respectfully no matter what because we have resolved to be a loving and respectful human being?

This raises an important question: Do we intend to do toward others what we expect them to do toward us? Will we be kind communicators because we expect others to be kind communicators with us?

Ryan Anderson, an intellectual who espouses traditional values on college campuses, encountered something quite sobering on this topic of civility. Luma Simm wrote about Ryan, saying,

[He] has had to bear more than his share of shaming and harassment. "His public appearances are now lightning rods for ideological malevolence of a kind without counterpart elsewhere on the spectrum," Eberstadt writes. This exchange between Anderson and a *New York Times* reporter moved me to tears:

"[While] Anderson repeatedly made the case for civility and respect for opposing perspectives, the reporter responded with, 'Why shouldn't I call you names?,' and 'Civility is not always a virtue,' and 'Some people are deserving of incivility,' and 'Obviously some policy views render people unworthy of respect.' Anderson explained, 'People are always worthy of respect, even if their policy views are misguided. Nothing renders people "unworthy of respect."' He continued: 'I think even when we vehemently disagree with someone the person still has innate human dignity, still worthy of respect.'"[3]

Is this *New York Times* reporter the new secular Pharisee who is self-righteous, angry, judgmental, and damning? Does he envision himself as having divine rights and someone like Ryan Anderson deserves stoning? This boggles the mind.

However, everyone, including this reporter, knows that incivility is wrong. How so? When the roles are reversed, the victimizer turned victim begs for mercy and justice. The formerly uncivil soul treated with incivility protests the hatred and contempt. "Unfair!" come the shouts. Why can't the *New York Times* reporter recognize this while he's spewing his hatred and contempt? He wants others to abide by the Golden Rule when communicating with him but refuses that right to Ryan Anderson.

I have observed this avoidance of the Golden Rule spilling over into marriages and daily communication as well.

One woman carried around a book in front of her husband with the title that said, in effect, "How to Live with an Evil Man." She did this because she was mad at him and wanted him to change, so she used uncivil treatment to motivate him to love her! Go figure! When he fumed in anger, it defeated her because it confirmed her deepest fears: "He doesn't love me." However, what would she feel if her husband carried around a book with the title, "How to Live with an Evil Wife"?

Though the end can be worthy (to be loved and respected), when each uses unholy means (unloving and disrespectful words and actions), it will not achieve those ends. We must treat others as we expect them to treat us. To deny this makes us arrogant or fools, or both.

Why Do We Communicate What Is Unkind?

Some of us would never consider lying. We are truthful communicators. However, we appear unkind. Others hear us speak or read what we write and conclude, "This person is neither loving nor respectful." Why this conclusion? We have our reasons for being unkind. Do any of these hit home?

THE BULLY: When I'm mean-spirited, it works. When I intimidate, I get my way.

THE RETALIATOR: I'm mean only when others are unkind to me; it's an eye for an eye.

THE BLUNT: I'm not harsh but brutally honest in telling others what they don't want to hear.

THE UNEMPATHETIC: I'm no teary-eyed hand-holder. The feeble need to toughen up.

THE IMPATIENT: I don't have time for polite greetings but need to get to my point.

THE VANQUISHER: To win, I'll lie and dishonor my competition. My end justifies my means.

THE RESENTER: I've been dishonored and treated unfairly. Yeah, I'm infuriated and gruff.

THE CONDITIONAL: People who don't earn my respect don't deserve it. Period.

THE DEFEATED: Showing kindness doesn't return kindness. It backfires. It must be me.

THE ENVIOUS: Life is unfair to me. I don't have what others do. Sure, I'm begrudging.

THE INTOLERANT: I detest and cannot stomach those who hold to beliefs at odds with mine.

THE UNMINDFUL: Truthfully, I'm preoccupied and inadvertently hurt others by my neglect.

THE UNINTENTIONAL: I didn't mean to be insensitive or coldhearted. I was just upset.

THE REBEL: I can't stand rules like being told to be kind. I'll be any way I wish to be.

THE DU JOUR: People need to get over it and get with it. This is how we now talk and text.

THE ANTI-SOCIAL: I want to be left alone, so I push people away. I don't want to be bothered.

THE DEAF: I think others are hearing things; I don't hear unkindness in my voice at all.

THE OFFSPRINGER: People need to chill out. This is how my family of origin reacts in conflict.

THE ABUSER: I'm not abusive, and whatever idiot says that better guard his back.

THE SELF-HATER: Stressed out, under-exercised, and overeating, I react. I don't like myself.

The Bully

It is difficult to argue against the bully's short-term experience. Bullying works. Telling your playmate to give you money or he'll end up with a bloody nose puts cash in the pocket. Getting some dirt on a trader on Wall Street and using that to gain insider trading enables one to buy a yacht.

We meanly raise our voices at local retailers, demanding a refund, and presto, it works. We meanly threaten divorce, and our spouses work on the marriage. We meanly tell the landlord we intend to sue because of the broken pipes, and he replaces the pipes and also paints our apartment.

We hit send on unkind communications because kindness gets less results than unkindness.

But every bully needs to ask, *Can I secure my wishes only via intimidation? Do I lack the confidence in my honorable character to appeal to others to provide what I need? Can I not use my good heart to motivate others? Do I need to yell at the retailer, threaten divorce, and scream litigation against the landlord?*

Quality people believe that their own characters and appealing to the good character in others best motivates people. Long term, as reputable citizens, we believe civility most effectively protects and advances our interests.

When people feel that we are loving and respectful souls, they move in our direction and seek to help us. Though that is not always true, as our bully proves, over time kind, loving, and respectful people influence others because others want to be influenced that way. Before we hit send we need to ask, *Will this correspondence, voice message, or over-the-counter discussion sound mean-spirited or courteous?*

The Retaliator

Retaliation is comparable to the sting of a honey bee. The stinger is barbed, so it cannot be pulled out. When the bee does try to pull, it pulls out its abdomen and digestive tract and dies from the rupture. Retaliation is our attempt to sting another. Even if we succeed at inflicting a mortal wound on the other, it ends in double graves.

What do we feel when an associate at work, in front of several others, makes an unkind remark about how horrible we look in the clothes we have on, and then adds, "But that's nothing compared to losing the Houston account." Humiliated, we immediately feel hurt and then anger. We want to hit back to even the score. Tit for tat. After all, we have our dignity, and hostility and contempt send the message: don't you dare treat me as you did the other day, or there is a price to pay.

But this "eye for an eye and tooth for a tooth" tendency reduces us to our associate's level. When we bite the snake, it doesn't change the character of the snake; it leaves people wondering what kind of person bites a snake.

To convict the other, we need to act on the wisdom of the ages. "But if your enemy is hungry, feed him, and if he is thirsty, give him a drink; for in so doing you will heap burning coals on his head" (Rom. 12:20). George Eliot wrote in *The Mill on the Floss*, "To see an enemy humiliated gives a certain contentment, but this is jejune compared with the highly blent satisfaction of seeing him humiliated by your benevolent action . . . That is the sort of revenge which falls into the scale of virtue."[4]

Before hitting send, can I answer that this is not rooted in retaliation? Evening the score will only keep the retaliation going. Another approach is to show a desire to empathize with the other person's needs. That can soften him or her and hopefully bring about mutual understanding concerning the issue rather than escalating attacks on each other.

The Blunt

One woman wrote to me, saying, "The truth is the truth . . . it really doesn't matter how you communicate it. The reaction in how the other person receives the truth lies in her ability or emotional frame of mind to receive it."

On the one hand, I grasp her point. Some are sitting on unresolved issues from childhood and that spills over onto us. We can communicate the truth in the best of manners, but the person may be so insecure he or she can only react and attack like a wounded bear.

On the other hand, sometimes we unlovingly dump the truth on people and blame them for not receiving it. We are harsh and don't see it. We claim we are brutally honest, but we are just brutal. We claim others are emotionally disabled when we lack graciousness in the way we communicate.

Though some who hear us are unteachable, some of us do not have a loving and respectful demeanor when writing or speaking. People shut down on us because we are blunt and rude, but we blind ourselves to how we communicate.

When others do not respond to our communication, we need to look first at our communication style. Is the other person incapable of hearing what we have to say? Or are we abrupt, brusque, and curt?

Do we see ourselves as some kind of honorable prosecutor who upholds the truth but are offensively impolite and ill-mannered? Do people feel indicted and accused by us? Do they feel we are putting them on trial? Are people on the defensive because we are offensive? Does this have little to do with truth and everything to do with our lack of love?

Dietrich Bonhoeffer wrote, "Truth without love is nothing—it is not even truth, for truth is God, and God is love. So truth without love is a lie; it is nothing."[5]

The Unempathetic

I know of one leader who held the viewpoint of the Unempathetic: "I am not going to spoon feed them like little children!" This comment became the straw that broke the camel's back, and he lost a half dozen of his loyal staff who felt defeated by his condescending posture. His attitude, displayed by his assessment, quenched their desires to serve him, and this was after many years of faithfully following him.

Such a view overstates the case as a way of excusing the call to be empathetic. When we can create a straw man of what an empathetic person ought to be, we can blow it over quite easily. An extreme caricature allows us to absolve ourselves from kindly listening to the need of the person in front of us. We claim that if we must bawl when others weep, then we must reject the expectation of comforting those in pain. After all, we don't bawl.

What it does reveal is that we have chosen to be insensitive and unaware. We profile people in need as needy. We characterize them as feeble, not us as unfeeling; as pathetic, not us as unempathetic. We interpret their true vulnerability as false victimhood. We contend that they pretend.

The truth is, when someone turns to you when she feels vulnerable, this is one of the greatest compliments to who you are. The person isn't asking you to fall down and cry your eyes out. Instead, she wishes for you to see through her eyes. That's what empathy is. Why profile this person as pitiful and weak when she turns to you and your strengths for understanding?

Most of those around us do not ask that we be responsible for them. Most are not looking for us to heal them but to understand their wounds. They are not looking for a hug but hope. They are not asking for us to be kin but kind.

The Unempathetic sometimes finds himself ready to hit send on an e-mail that appears kind, but he refuses to do so because he envisions an empathetic communication to mean he has become a teary-eyed, hand-holding turncoat. And if he's not that, the other person will see him as being more understanding and want a greater emotional connection, and that must be avoided.

The Impatient

Jumping right in on our urgent point is okay to do when the relationship is solid. However, if the other person does not have a relationship with us, he or she will most likely interpret our to-the-point remarks as abrupt and then seek to decipher the tone. Human nature is such that most interpret abruptness as the communicator feeling negative or indifferent.

"But, Emerson, must I be concerned with politeness when the other tested my patience by causing the problem?" We should not forget the old saying, "You can catch more flies with honey than with vinegar." Sour, impolite demands won't achieve our ends better than

---

politeness, not long term where we live in community. For example, what does the worker in the accounting department at Peterson's Oil Company think of this e-mail? **To whom it may concern: You over charged me by $175. You got it wrong. Here is my account number. Get it right and make it right.**

This is not an evil e-mail; nonetheless, I predict the worker will conclude the sender is miffed. When we blurt out what we feel is unfair, the hearer assumes we are ticked. Why not write instead,

> Maybe an honest oversight occurred here, but I was overcharged $175. Am I missing the reason for this? Please let me know what happened. If someone could look into this, I'd be appreciative. I know you are busy. If it would make it easier for you, credit that to my next month's bill. Thank you for helping me.

Do we actually think that the first approach achieves our ends better than the second approach? All of this returns to the Golden Rule. If the roles here were reversed, we would deeply appreciate the second approach and respond. Yes, it would demand of the person to patiently write seven sentences, not four; but the "honey" method would catch our attention, and this patient demeanor would free us up to admit and correct our mistake.

The Vanquisher

Baseball manager Leo Durocher was reportedly the first to say, "Nice guys finish last."[6] Winning demands toughness. But some add ruthlessness. Some adhere to the idea that in order to win there is to be no pity or compassion. One may need to be cruel, mean and demeaning, mad and mouthy. Whatever it takes, they intend to come out on top. To them, it's dog eat dog.

However, nice guys do win. Just ask Peyton and Eli, NFL quarterbacks. Although Peyton is now retired, the Manning brothers have won a lot. If we are decent, friendly, and agreeable, we can still win. We can vanquish fairly by our superior play.

What is interesting is that when people cannot win on the merits of their performance, products, or positions, they are tempted to cross a line and speak horribly of the opponent, perhaps even lying. Former presidential candidate Dr. Ben Carson said, "Intelligent people tend to talk about the facts. They don't sit around and call each other names. That's what you can find on a third-grade playground."[7] But as many wish to agree with Ben, many see the name-callers winning. Mud-slinging does bring victory. So it comes down to the type of person I will be.

We all must ask ourselves individually, *Will I compromise my character and the truth in order to win? Will I succeed no matter the cost?* For those of us who know what is right and good, *Will I live by the light I possess? Will I remain true to who I am or will I go over to the dark side like Darth Vader?* That does not mean every decision is an easy one to make. There are gray areas. But consciously and willfully we will not falsely call people evil and do evil so we can cross the line first. We will not deceptively dishonor the competition. That's not a victory, that's a vice.

The Resenter

Having listened to the stories of people, I have been amazed at the evil—yes, evil—some have been subjected to. Life isn't fair. I met a gentleman, tortured for years by a communist regime, who endured iron hooks through the skin on his back as he hung from the rafters. Several women have reported to me the sexual abuse that came to them as innocent, naive, and precious little girls.

What strikes me about these particular people is that they did not become bitter but better. No gruffness. The unanswered questions and injustice of life did not cause them to become resentful and unkind individuals.

What I find peculiar is when others in lesser situations turn resentful toward any and all. They blame God and others. God did not allow them to be born into a rich and beautiful family. Or they had to take two years off from college to work since their parents could not fund their education.

In all of these circumstances, nothing evil happened. Instead, they didn't get what they wanted and turned bitter. They turned cynical and see everyone intending to mistreat them, unless given proof to the contrary. Most often they dish it out first before anybody has a chance to mistreat them. E-mails manifest a chip on the shoulder. Texts have a negative, unkind edge. Phone calls are unpleasant. All of this is to protect self but only causes people to profile them as resentful and gruff.

Might this describe you? Have you become a verbal flamethrower? Are you infuriated by past injustices, some of which have been evil, but you have turned bitter and take it out on people who have never wronged you? Does unkindness permeate your communication with the people around you because you have been stepped on by individuals many years ago? Is this who you want to be? Sometimes the most sensitive turn insensitive and do toward others what was done to them—which is an amazing irony. Those who have been dishonored earlier in life turn unloving and gruff to prevent further hurts. But dishonoring others does not lead to honor.

The Conditional

When we deem another person as not having earned our respect, does this give us license to show him or her disrespect in our texts, tweets, e-mails, and on Facebook? A person wrote to me once, saying,

> Respect was not something I learned in my childhood. My parents have a very verbally destructive marriage so I learned well how to be ugly with my voice and words. I learned that respect is earned. Either you work hard to earn it or you don't. Needless to say, others never worked hard enough in my eyes to earn an ounce of respect from me.

When we have the attitude that we are fully justified in showing others disrespect, because they have failed our standard, what makes us think they will respond to us long term? I can win this round with them by using my disrespect to manipulate them, but what about tomorrow and next week and next month. Disrespect doesn't influence hearts.

In today's world we need to keep two groups with whom we communicate in mind. Group one consists of people in our lives. Group two consists of people "out there," like those on the Internet. Some of us let down our civil guard toward people "out there." But to the extent that we show contempt toward politicians, businesses, authors, celebrities, and the religious, not only do we prove ineffective, but this attitude also spills over onto our everyday interactions with people in our personal world. We cannot think we can treat those "out there" with contempt without it having any bearing on our daily interactions. The truth is, we are who we are. This disrespectful demeanor inevitably shows up at work, when dating, in our families, and among neighbors.

This isn't about others being worthy of respect; this is about us communicating our message respectfully even if the other doesn't deserve it. This is unconditional respect, which seems like a contradiction of terms but simply means being a respectful person regardless of another's actions. Does this mean we give others license to do whatever they selfishly demand? No. Unconditional respect means we confront their wrongdoings respectfully. We do not become uncivil because they are. Who they fail to be does not determine who we will be.

The Defeated

When others do not respond to our kindness, some of us move into self-deprecation and doubt. "It must be me. There must be something inherently wrong with me. I will stop trying to be so kind."

Charlie Brown famously told us in *Peanuts*, "Nothing takes the taste out of peanut butter quite like unrequited love."[8] Any time we are genuinely kind, loving, and respectful and are ignored, we feel kicked in the gut. Some of us blame ourselves. We did something wrong—again. However, we have to be mature adults who exercise discernment. If everything we did was truly loving and respectful, we cannot conclude that something is wrong with us simply because the love was not returned.

You cared for your dad, but he did not appreciate your efforts and actually reacted negatively. Does that mean you are a horrible adult child? Or is this your dad's issue? Sarah, my wife, and I have often stopped and asked, on the heels of being mistreated by a family member, "Is this our issue or their issue?" We have to be honest. Sometimes it is the other person's problem, so we are not going to despise ourselves because he or she gives off the air that we are the ones with the problem. I say this because some kind people take the blame inappropriately.

Why quit your job because two associates repaid all the overtime you put in for them with an arrogant and false claim in their report that they did all the work? You didn't want the recognition anyway. Why let their disgraceful actions cause you to punish yourself by quitting your employment in a company of fifty others who highly esteem you? Why let the lies of two people override the sentiments of the vast majority? Stay the course. When your kindness goes unrewarded, you must not turn unkind and defeated. There are irregular people out there, and this is their problem, not your issue.

The Envious

Envy is desiring what another has and being discontent with what we have. You say to your husband, "I wish you made more money so we could have a house like the Andersons have." Or you discover your colleague just received a pay increase and bonus, and you have to hold back from giving your boss a piece of your mind.

Such envy is selective in what it sees when another possesses more. If all the offices are without windows, we do not envy other workers. Let a skylight come to a peer, and now we feel envy. Something comes over us. Also, we envy others' rewards, not their risks; the pleasure, not their pain; their successes, not their sacrifices. We are selective.

I heard a person confront an envious soul with, "You want what they now have, but you didn't want to go through what they went through to get what they now have." Sure, the medical doctor living next door may have a new Mercedes, but do not forget his twelve years of living a dollar above poverty while in medical school and residency, or his four hours of sleep every night for a decade.

Another thought. Why envy others when our condition is the result of the good choices we made? Often we are where we are because we chose to be in this situation. We are not victims. For instance, we married who we did for love, not for money. We could've chased after someone with wealth, but that's not what we wanted then, and we really don't want it now. We must remind ourselves of our choices. To conquer envy, we must revisit why we are where we are.

We must also recognize that people have their struggles. Ironically, the woman in the luxury home envies the love of her friend's husband and four children. A Danish proverb says, "If envy were a fever, all the world would be ill."[9]

"But, Emerson, what if another gets what he doesn't deserve and I don't get what I do deserve?" For example, we deserve the promotion and pay increase but due to prejudice against us, we lose what is rightfully ours. Or what if the other wife down the street has the love of a husband and a ton of money in the bank, and we have no money from an embezzlement and our husbands have stopped loving us? Martin Luther King Jr. understood this injustice: "I have a dream that my four little children will one day live in a nation where they will not be judged by the color of their skin but by the content of their character."[10] What did Dr. King suggest we do? "Darkness cannot drive out darkness; only light can do that. Hate cannot drive out hate; only love can do that."[11] When life is unfair, the person of character moves forward as Dr. King modeled.

Letting envy create nasty and complaining communications will not lead to a rescue from those who read what we write or hear what we speak. Instead, they'll hit delete on our e-mails and cross to the other side when they see us on the street.

The Intolerant

We are free to reject the beliefs we deem false. But civil people do not have a right nor desire to hate those who adhere to systems of belief they find abhorrent. Civility does not mean we sanction their "truth claims." However, to bring them out of their false persuasion, we must show them love and respect. If we do not, we will not win their hearts. Furthermore, we sour them to what we believe. When we detest people, they will not listen from the heart to the truth claims of our faith. Why would they wish to hear from someone who wishes them dead?

When we tweet vile comments about those who differ and wish to silence them, legally or through violence, we subscribe to the philosophy that says, "When I deem you wrong, you lose all rights." That, of course, only shows the weakness of our own position. I have said over the years, "Let any religion or philosophy be preached alongside of me as I preach Jesus Christ. I do not fear their position. I have confidence in the message of Jesus Christ. But when others silence me in favor of their own positions, then I know they lack the confidence in their own faith or philosophy as having a stand-alone appeal."

Those who are kind and show respect evidence a contentment and confidence in what they believe. Those who silence or kill others show just how fearful they are that they are wrong in their supposed truth claims. They are intolerant because they fear hearing something that might undermine their faith perspective. This does not mean we let others control our individual faith communities, only that in the public square we do not show hate, contempt, and violence. Truth carries its own weight, and we should feel confident about this. When we yield to "might makes right," there is something inherently wrong in what we believe, and we know it.

All of us must adhere to the idea that we will debate against the views of others while defending their right to hold these views. Our Founding Fathers subscribed to the belief that one's own liberty is not safe until the other person's liberty is guarded.

The Unmindful

The husband forgets his anniversary, as his wife waits at home for him. The teen forgets to call home, leaving the parents fearful for a short period. The manager forgets to cancel the meeting, and several people show up.

Preoccupation makes us unmindful of very practical things.

Few who are preoccupied intend to be unloving and

disrespectful. We can be absorbed in other important matters. The husband who forgets his anniversary can be engrossed in solving an insurance problem of a client, doing so with a compassionate concern to help. The manager can be working on a health package for his employees, doing so with such obsession he forgets they are waiting down the hall for him. The teen is a teen out having fun, that's all. As one thing takes up our attention, it distracts us from something else. We've all been there.

It isn't what we say that is unkind but what we don't say that proves unkind. The enemy of the good is not always the bad but our failure to do what is the best. When others have a need for our kind communication and we neglect them, we hurt them. A sin of commission can sometimes be less painful than a sin of omission. A child shouting "I hate you" is less painful to the parent than a parent never saying "I love you" to the child.

A man said to me once, "My wife complains to me about our marriage. But I am home every evening. I don't go out drinking, and there are no other women." His argument reminds me of the husband who declares, "I do not beat my wife." That's great, but do you love her, and does she feel that love? Beating a wife is the sin of commission. Failing to love her in meaningful ways is the sin of omission.

Some of us are horrible communicators, and it has

nothing to do with what we say. It has everything to do with what we don't say.

The Unintentional

Most of us do not intend to hurt other people. But because our unkind words slip out without ill will does not mean other people should let the verbal bullets bounce off them like marshmallows. When I accidentally spill hot water on the person sitting next to me, he or she is still scalded.

Hurting in her marriage and threatened by a spouse demanding space and time alone, a wife communicates on her Facebook page, **Pray for me. My unbelieving husband is leaving me. I think there is another woman.** He reads her Facebook comment in shock. "I did not say I am leaving you, and there is no other woman. I am just feeling disrespected in this home and have lost energy by comments like these that you put out to the world." Quickly apologizing, she voices, "I was wrong. Please forgive me. I was just upset and not in my right mind."

Being overlooked the second time for a promotion, in the boardroom we lambaste the company for its fast-track policies that advance certain ethnic groups above others. Called out by management, we seek to retrack our blistering comments. "I was just upset. I didn't intend to hurt anybody."

Unkind words scald. Whether accidental or intentional, the effects are pretty much the same.

But here's the real challenge. Do we frequently find ourselves saying, "I didn't mean it the way it came across. I wasn't trying to be insensitive and coldhearted, it just appeared that way"? When a person spills hot water repeatedly and claims it was accidental, those around no longer believe in the innocence of the claim.

When we are regularly apologizing for unkind speaking, we need to step back and consider if the onus is on the other person to understand us or if we need better self-understanding. Because we did not intend to be mean doesn't mean we are not mean—if you know what I mean.

The Rebel

Some of us declare, "It's my life. I make the rules. Keep your nose out of my affairs." At one level such independence is commendable and noble. No one wants your codependency. But what occurs when you say to another, "If I wish to communicate unkindly to you, I will, and it's none of your business"? Soon enough it becomes my business. You are not the only rebel in the world, and when you speak rudely to me, you cross a line; you violate a basic rule. Hayden Fry, football coach at Iowa, said, "In football, like in life, you must learn to play within the rules of the game."[12]

Unkindness is outside the rules of engagement.

When a woman rebels against the idea of showing respect to her husband when addressing matters that feel unloving to her, she predictably will appear disdainful toward who he is. At that juncture her husband shuts down emotionally and pulls away. He won't connect with her heart-to-heart. In fact, at that moment no husband would have fond feelings of love and affection toward a wife he thinks despises who he is as a human being.

Yet there are mutinous women who scream at this idea of respecting their husbands (Eph. 5:33; 1 Peter 3:1–2), rebelling like sailors ready to throw the captain of the ship overboard. Instead of accepting this rule of engagement—that a man softens and moves toward his wife to connect with her as his best friend when he senses she believes in him and respects him as a person created in the image of God—she kicks into a mantra of rebellion. "I don't feel respect and won't be a hypocrite in showing respect when I don't feel it. Respect is earned, not given." Of course, contempt is her only alternative, and no human being responds positively to contempt, so her point is lost on him. Instead of seeing respect as meeting a husband's need, apart from his performance—as she has a need to be treated with respect apart from her failings as a wife— she arches her back in fearful rebellion as though she will lose her identity and power as a woman if she confronts her husband respectfully. She rebels against these rules of engagement because she feels she is being told she must be a doormat, not a welcome mat. "Whatever," she complains, "I will be a mat and walked on."

Perhaps it is the word *rule* that ignites your ire. What if we quoted Franklin D. Roosevelt, who said, "Rules are not necessarily sacred; principles are"?[13]

When we consider as sacred the commitment to be kind, loving, and respectful, we are operating on a sacred principle. Doesn't it make sense to speak the necessary truth kindly and clearly to others? This is about being a person of principle. How can that be an oppressive and totalitarian idea? The rebel needs to be honest with himself. This is far less about being controlled by others and more about being out of self-control.

The Du Jour

Emily Post said, "Manners are a sensitive awareness of the feelings of others. If you have that awareness, you have good manners, no matter what fork you use."[14]

Some find it ridiculous to always try to communicate with a huge awareness of and sensitivity to the feelings of others. At one level this is understandable. Some are triggered emotionally by the smallest of offenses. However, not a few communicators today find it publicly popular to speak abusively of those they deem wrong on any number of issues. This is the soup of the day, and they intend to serve it. Instead of seeing their poor verbal manners as a mirror of the kind of people they are, they think they are better than this other person who as a lesser human being deserves their coarse comments.

"But, Emerson, there is the expression, 'Full of courtesy, full of craft.'" I agree. There is a syrupy politeness that covers over the subversive agenda. We are not recommending false and superficial manners but true and sincere manners. We are recommending the cessation of coarse talking and texting and always communicating in ways that sound loving and respectful. Ultimately, this is the most effective way of persuading and affecting hearts.

I appeal to you to be the type of person that you would turn to if in a predicament. The type of people who are always dropping the F bomb as the subject, verb, and object not only show their limited vocabulary but also appear angry. Do folks turn to such people in crisis? Do you? Vocabulary reveals the heart, according to Jesus (Matt. 12:34).

Much of this over-the-top language is popular today, but it will be short-lived. Avoid giving in to the du jour of texting and tweeting coarse language. By way of analogy, I envision people with tattoos all over their wrinkled bodies as they sit in wheelchairs at age ninety-two. What seems normal now will appear quite abnormal then. I have a friend who got a tattoo during WWII, a very popular thing to do. He had it removed in midlife. Some things prove to be out of place.

Unkind, rude, ill-mannered language may be avant-garde for a season but not for a lifetime. What is profanely popular to utter will soon be seen as nothing but the gutter. When we have children who follow our example of profanity and drop the F bomb, we change our word choices. Language matters, and we know it.

Old-fashioned manners may be old, but they are still in fashion.

The Anti-Social

A work associate invites us to a social gathering at her home. Do we ignore her e-mail instead of graciously declining? When we tire of another socially, do we unfriend him by removing him from a list of friends on our social network instead of just leaving well enough alone? Do we block our mothers and fathers from e-mailing us as a way of declaring they are harassing us when the truth is we don't want to maturely engage them on making arrangements for Thanksgiving and Christmas at Grandma's house?

Is not wanting to spend time socially with others always a horrible thing? Some of us who are introverts need to get away from the crowd. We feel suffocated and de-energized. Audrey Hepburn said, "I have to be alone very often. I'd be quite happy if I spent from Saturday night until Monday morning alone in my apartment. That's how I refuel."[15] Refueling to reengage with people is most understandable and acceptable.

But that differs from getting time alone by being unkind to people, pushing them away. In a bizarre way, some use rudeness as a method to ensure solitude and avoid the social demand to be friendly.

Being true to one's shy temperament does not demand hate and contempt toward others to ensure breathing room. Why de-energize others who are more social by pushing them away in order to gain energy for ourselves? We can find win–win, not win–lose. What right do we have to serve ourselves by depriving others of their right to receive something from us?

For example, we notice a neighbor at a restaurant on Saturday morning, so we seek seating on the opposite side in a booth out of sight. That might be appropriate, but we need to prepare ourselves to be a bit more social in a public setting. Entering a public place increases the chances of seeing someone or being seen, and it takes too much energy to always be jumping behind bushes. In seeing someone you know, you need to be prepared to say hi and ask how the other person is doing, while standing there, and then move to your seat. If the person asks you to join him or her, don't feel guilty in declining graciously. Just say, "Thanks for the invitation, but I'm going to grab a quiet booth and collect my thoughts (or read the paper, read a book, clear out my text messages or my e-mail, or whatever) this morning. But thank you so much for the invitation; you are kind to ask." Most people respect our reasons since they themselves have been in a similar situation. Though we are saying no, we are seeking to be courteous while being truthful. There is no need to blurt out, "No. I can't sit with you. I have other things to do." The message is the same, but it is self-focused and ignores honoring the other person. The neighbor is made to feel as though he or she is out of line for asking. Sadly, this is sometimes the intent of the anti-social. "Honestly, I wanted to abruptly shut the door on the invitation so he'd leave me alone."

The Deaf

Do people ask you, "Are you angry about something?" Does a family member ask, "What did you mean in that e-mail? Do you love me?" Does an associate ask, "From the voice message, I get the feeling you are peeved. Are you?"

These questions may provide a clue that we are deaf to our tone even if we mean no unkindness. If we are constantly replying to others, "I didn't mean it the way it sounded to you," then we have a problem in what we voice and what we write.

When it comes to our face-to-face interactions, a great

question to ask ourselves is this: *Would a blind person be attracted to us?* Blind people hear the tone of our voices, our word choices, and the gentle touch of our hands. They have no idea what we look like. A drop-dead gorgeous movie star might get away with sounding unkind and disrespectful to others, but a blind person would be turned off to her. What's a pretty face to a blind person?

Do we hear ourselves? A person said to me, "Several commented that I sounded like I was complaining and criticizing. They said that I had a disrespectful tone. But I didn't mean it that way. I don't get it. Why would they misinterpret my heart when I care?"

Some of us are good-hearted, caring individuals, but for a variety of reasons, we are deaf to our tone of unkindness. It could be our deep voices and matter-of-fact way of communicating that makes others feel we are mad, our high-pitched shrills and shrieks that make others feel attacked and on edge, or our blunt writing that makes others feel we lack compassion and empathy. There is a discrepancy between who we want to be and see ourselves to be and how we actually sound in voice and writing. But with self-reflection and honesty, we can turn the corner and improve our communication. We need only evaluate what we are about to communicate. *Will this be heard or read as loving and respectful or will the other person incorrectly read between the lines that I am peeved?*

The words we are saying are only half of our communication. The other half is what others are hearing. Will we hear what they hear? Or will we obstinately claim, "They are hearing things"?

The Offspringer

Not a few families deal with their issues by yelling and screaming at one another, and then they feel better for a while until the next altercation. Or some shut down in anger until it works out of their system, but they avoid ever talking about the conflict.

Whether we are talking about outbursts of anger or a total shutdown, this is not the kind, loving, and respectful way of resolving serious tensions. Unfortunately, as adults, this way of dealing with conflicts and stresses in our families of origin spills over into everyday living at school, work, YMCA, church, or wherever.

Sadly, we make an excuse. "Sorry. This is how I am. This is how my family deals with conflict. You need to chill out. I am angry, but soon enough I am over it. Don't take it so personally even though, at the moment, I'm taking it out on you. Give me some time, and I'll move on. I'll be good to go."

I am one who could've used that excuse. I saw my dad attempt to strangle my mom. Years later, there were moments that I could feel anger rise in me, the anger I saw in my dad. But I was determined not to be like Dad. I consciously said, "I will not be like Dad."

A man wrote to me, "I was not good at responding to someone when they expressed anger. My mother had used rage and anger to control me as I was growing up. Therefore, I would interpret any raised and loud voice as someone expressing anger toward me. Especially women. Someone was either mad, upset, or disappointed with me. I would respond by either shutting down or I would retaliate back with anger."

I do not minimize the predispositions we have from our families of origin. That is inescapable at one level. However, predispositions must never be interpreted as predestinations. We are not destined to explode or implode because our moms and dads did, and we do not have to treat others the way our parents treated us. We must not buy that lie. We are free to take a new course, and must.

Furthermore, to tell others to chill out puts the onus on them to change. No, we need to change. Our default reaction from childhood is a defect from childhood. Our family-of-origin reactions don't serve as an explanation but as an excuse. The sooner we own up to this, the sooner we will be more effective communicators. People don't buy the offspring excuse. They just see us as off, and putting them off.

The Abuser

The verbal and emotional abuser often is blind to his abuse, mostly because the abuse he is guilty of isn't physical. One strikes not with fists but with words that leave emotional wounds and scars. But verbal abuse also shows how empty and unconvincing one feels about the stand-alone merits of the concern. One does not believe that loving and respectful words will carry the message. One must turn toxic to disparage and defame. One turns heartless and vicious.

Often the abuser is feeling insecure, inadequate, or rejected. Verbal abuse empowers. The abuser, though, has lost touch with the root issue, which often is the feeling of being unloved and disrespected.

The bagger at the grocery store accidentally drops one of our bags with four wine bottles that we had special ordered three weeks earlier. All four smash on the blacktop. Enraged, we curse at him. Later we go on Yelp to write a review:

> The service at Pine Hills Grocery is always horrid. I have no idea who oversees the workers, but this manager has a working disability. Every bagger drops bags, every cashier gives back the wrong change in the store's favor, and every shelf is plastered with Out of Stock signs. This manager needs to take his store and shelve it!

Fixated on mistakes, we globalize to "every" and "always." From there we conclude this staff doesn't care about us. So we spew venom. Our harsh rhetoric evens the score and ensures change.

My conjecture is that at the root you feel unloved and disrespected—probably erroneously—and speak abusive words of hate and contempt. Do you see this in yourself? George MacDonald penned, "A beast does not know that he is a beast, and the nearer a man gets to being a beast the less he knows it."[16]

The Self-Hater

A woman who struggled with weight gain wrote,

> I was depressed. I hated myself both for how I looked and for letting myself get that way. . . . Self hatred and fear of intimacy was taking a toll. . . . But this didn't inspire me to start cutting back on snacks or start jogging. No, I just ate more snacks while I felt sorry for myself.

All of this undermined her relationships with others. Hating herself prevented her from loving and honoring others. She was totally self-focused. Our hearts go out to her in her struggles.

However, for some, it is more than a bad attitude toward others because they feel overweight. For some, self-hate turns to outward hate. They react harshly and with hostility toward others because of their self-loathing. Obviously, this harms the relationship. The other person is clueless and pulls away. In fact, it creates enemies. "You hate me; then I'll hate you." Round and round it goes, and all the worse when both struggle with self-disgust. Added to the mix are those individuals suffering from horrendous guilt over past transgressions. Feeling hopeless, why not spew out venom at others? "No one would respect me anyway if they knew the true me and what I have done."

One wonders if the many who lash out on social media may actually hate themselves. Yes, they are upset about some issue, but it goes deeper. Having no self-respect, they show no respect. Having no self-love, they communicate no love. They hurt others by their unkind words because they are hurting.

Here's the point: when the circumstances in our lives—whatever they may be—cause us to hate and disrespect ourselves, we will react to others in unkind ways. How sad that we claim others tick us off when it is actually ourselves who are the culprits. We feel stressed, unhealthy, and fat, or worse. We can't stand ourselves but appear as though we can't stand others.

Why Should We Communicate
What Is Kind?

We should take all the reasons why we communicate unkindly and reverse them. People respond positively to those who refuse to be unempathetic, impatient, resentful, envious, intolerant, unmindful, and anti-social or the bully, retaliator, self-appointed prosecutor, rebel, and abuser. Even so, there are three good reasons why we should communicate kindly. It's about who I am, who the other person is, and who God is.

My communicating kindly demonstrates who I am. As we have frequently quoted, Jesus said the mouth speaks out of that which fills the heart. Kind speech shows us as a kind person. Other people may be undeserving of the kind speech, but they cannot force us to become like them. They cannot get us to hate them. That's not who we are.

We are not puppets manipulated by others' mistreatments. Though they may negatively affect our hearts, and hurt us, they do not control our words and actions. We are not under their spell. We are free at our core. Our response is our right and is under our rule. They do not cause our responses; they only reveal our reactions. When we step on a rose, the sweet aroma ascends to our nostrils. When we step on a skunk, a different aroma ascends. Did the stepping on both cause the aroma, or did it reveal the inner properties of the rose and skunk? When others step on us, they reveal who we are.

My communicating kindly recognizes others are created in God's image, and I respond accordingly. It makes no difference if I am writing an e-mail, texting, tweeting, talking on the phone, or meeting in person; when the other person feels an undercurrent of disdain, he or she becomes guarded if not totally closed off.

PEOPLE DO NOT RECEIVE A HATEFUL AND CONTEMPTUOUS MESSAGE. God did not create people to be receptive to the likes of this. When we ever so slightly pepper a communication with the message, "I find you repulsive and can't stand you," we kill the interaction. Even though 95 percent of the communication is helpful and healthy, a little leaven leavens the whole. A 160-pound person need only ingest .5 grams of cyanide to make his death nearly certain. One line of contempt kills most communication. This explains why some are so effective at communicating. They guard with their lives against that 5 percent.

Kindness and gentleness turn away wrath. Kindness softens the other's unkindness. Many have heard Proverbs 15:1 quoted: "A gentle answer turns away wrath."

A friend of the family went to a beautiful public area to take photographs. After taking pictures for several minutes, a man came charging from his home, screaming,

"Get off this property, or I will call the police. Leave! Now!" Stunned, our friend felt the impulse to holler back. She told me, "I was ready to speak first, think second. I wanted to shout, 'This is public property, and what right do you have to say what you just said?!'" Instead, she quickly apologized and said, "We didn't know. We will leave immediately. We are so sorry." The man instantly quieted down and said, "Okay, then, you can stay. No problem." The man then told her it was public property, and she could be there anytime. His reaction was based on kids frequenting the place and doing drugs. She told me, "What the Bible says about a gentle answer turning away wrath is so true."

KINDNESS EASES OTHERS, WHICH ENABLES THEM TO HEAR THE SUBSTANCE OF OUR CONCERN. A person wrote, "When I share something with (another), whether it is a hard, confrontational issue or something minor and I see their countenance fall, I ask 'Did I come across as disrespectful to you? I didn't mean to. I'm sorry. I have the highest respect for you.' That usually diffuses the situation . . . For (the other person), I've noticed that they are quicker to come to me and say sorry after they've had an angry outburst."

I believe people need love and respect just as they need air to breathe. Imagine everyone you speak to being hooked up to an oxygen tank marked "Love & Respect." We can be sure others will not be receptive to what we say when we step on their air hoses. At that juncture, the root problem isn't the topic; the issue is their feeling that we do not have a kind spirit toward them. They will listen with half an ear.

KINDNESS DEMONSTRATES AND BUILDS TRUST. I remember hearing in a college class, "You can help yourself a lot if you ask yourself before speaking, 'Is what I am about to say going to build trust or undermine trust in the relationship?'" From that I realized a couple of things. One, I had a responsibility to come across in a way that built trust. It didn't just happen. Two, when I did speak in ways that built trust, like sounding loving and respectful, only then would the other feel motivated to be receptive to what I had to say. When we couldn't care less about treating others with kindness, we should not scratch our heads in confusion when it dawns on us that people do not enjoy being around us or listening to us.

KINDNESS AFFECTS THE EMOTIONS, WHICH IS KEY WHEN SEEKING TO INFORM OR PERSUADE. Carl Jung wrote, "One looks back with appreciation to the brilliant teachers, but with gratitude to those who touched our human feelings."[17]

Something as simple as a note of affirmation goes a long way. A person who no longer worked for me sent a note of encouragement that affected my emotions, which kept her on my radar for future employment. She wrote:

"This is just a short message wishing you the best on the release of your new book. Hope God blesses you and your family so you can continue with your wonderful work! Best regards, N." That note touched my emotions, creating appreciation and motivation to rehire her.

KINDNESS MAINTAINS A RELATIONSHIP, AND RELATIONSHIP DETERMINES RESPONSE. What burns bridges between individuals? Let's illustrate with an experience I had with another person who wished to be hired by me for some short-term projects. We had some great interactions, but I decided on a different course.

Suddenly, I heard from him. He expressed to me that he was annoyed at the turn of events in my not hiring him. He felt the job was in the bag. He claimed he gave me more information than he normally would because he felt he had the job.

His statement that he was annoyed turned me off immediately. I also felt bad for him that he did not word himself differently. Why not say to me, "Oh, how disappointed I am in this turn of events. I was so excited to work on this project for you. I am truly sad. Actually, I presumed too much and provided more than I usually do. But I hope what I offered will prove helpful. If there is anything I failed to do that caused this turn of events, I welcome the feedback. I certainly would appreciate it if you'd rank my performance. Thank you!"

That verbal response would have provided an incentive for me to consider him for the future. He would have been building, not burning, a bridge.

Relationship determines response. When we are annoyed and express annoyance, we send the message that we find the other person wrong and unacceptable. Maybe he or she is. But if it is an honest difference of opinion, in a gray area, we need to tread lightly if we wish to maintain a meaningful relationship.

MY COMMUNICATING KINDLY DEMONSTRATES WHO GOD IS. According to Jesus, God the Father is kind toward us. So how can we be unkind to others? It is as simple as that. Yes, He is perfect and we are not, and we fail where He never fails, but He also calls us to imitate Him.

There is a major principle Jesus unfolds in His teaching: treat others as God treats you. For example, we are repeatedly called to forgive others because Christ has forgiven us. A compelling reason to communicate kindly to others has little to do with the other person and everything to do with us seeing this person affording us the opportunity to follow God's example to us.

A person wrote, "One question I was asking God was 'How can you show love and respect toward a hurtful person who is mean or indifferent?' The Lord spoke to my heart, 'I've been there, I know how you feel and I died for you. I did this toward you.' Oh my, what a revelation.

This was not an issue of whether someone treated me correctly but was I looking at this whole relationship the way God does, and treating this person as God treats me?"

Another rich dimension is that God is present and we can trust Him during tough moments. I have encouraged people to hear the call of Christ to do what we do unto Him. Jesus said that as we have done it to the least of these we have done it unto Him. I create the image of Jesus standing beyond the other's shoulder. One person wrote, "The image of myself looking through the other person and seeing Christ was exactly what I needed to hear. Knowing that when I hold my tongue and have self-control over my responses, it is not only out of love and respect for the other person but also in obedience to God. What a breakthrough! Duh! For me to be reminded that my awesome and mighty God is looking straight back at me when I'm saying unkind words . . . was what I needed to hear."

How Can We Respond to Others Who Communicate What Is Unkind?

- TO THE BULLY ("When I'm mean-spirited, it works. When I intimidate, I get my way."), say, "Is intimidation the only way you can secure what you want? I think you lack confidence in your honorable character to motivate me."

- TO THE RETALIATOR ("I'm mean only when others are unkind to me; it's an eye for an eye."), say,

    "Please forgive me for any unkindness. That wasn't intended. But your reaction feels like punishment way beyond my crime. Am I reading you the wrong way?"

- TO THE BLUNT ("I'm not harsh but brutally honest in telling others what they don't want to hear"), say,

    "I can be defensive and hypersensitive. Guilty as charged. But you can be offensive. Not to exaggerate but truth without love is comparable to heart surgery without anesthesia."

- TO THE UNEMPATHETIC ("I'm no teary-eyed hand-holder. The feeble need to toughen up."), say,

    "I turn to you since I value your understanding. I'm not playing the 'poor me' card. I'm not trying to be pathetic when I turn to you for help."

- TO THE IMPATIENT ("I don't have time for polite greetings but need to get to my point."), say,

    "Before you get right to your point, could you give me a heads-up on your feelings? I don't want to misread that you're disgruntled about me."

- TO THE VANQUISHER ("To win, I'll lie and dishonor my competition. My end justifies my means."), say,

"I have no problem with competition. Both of us are the better for it. But success without honor is success without significance. Is it wrong for me to expect you to be honorable?"

- TO THE RESENTER ("I've been dishonored and treated unfairly. Yeah, I'm infuriated and gruff."), say,

    "How can you be offended over unkindness from others and not expect me to be offended by your unkindness? Isn't this a bit dishonoring and unfair to me?"

- TO THE CONDITIONAL ("People who don't earn my respect don't deserve it. Period."), say,

    "The culture shouts, 'Respect is earned!' Okay, but what happens when someone hasn't earned it? Showing contempt won't motivate the heart to change."

- TO THE DEFEATED ("Showing kindness doesn't return kindness. It backfires. It must be me."), say,

    "Your kindness reflects who you are independent of others. If they show a cold heart to your warm heart, that's their issue, not your failure."

- TO THE ENVIOUS ("Life is unfair to me. I don't have what others do. Sure, I'm begrudging."), say,

    "I agree. It can feel unfair when others have more. But don't let that cause you to become a mean-spirited person. None have everything they want, and we all have more than we deserve."

- TO THE INTOLERANT ("I detest and cannot stomach those who hold to beliefs at odds with mine."), say,

    "We are free to reject beliefs we deem are false. But we shouldn't hate the people who believe them. We won't win their hearts, and we'll only sour them to our claims of what is truth."

- TO THE UNMINDFUL ("Truthfully, I'm preoccupied and inadvertently hurt others by my neglect."), say,

    "Rejoice that you're not mean-spirited. But don't be like the guy who says, 'I never beat my wife,' when the real problem is that he never shows that he loves her."

- TO THE UNINTENTIONAL ("I didn't mean to be insensitive or coldhearted. I was just upset."), say,

    "I relate. I have those moments too. But the inadvertent leap from being hurt to being hurtful is still unkindness. Take some time to think before you react."

- TO THE REBEL ("I can't stand rules like being told to be kind. I'll be any way I wish to be."), say,

    "When authoritarian people create unjust rules, question authority. But the rule to speak with kindness is a good one because hostility and contempt don't work long term."

- TO THE DU JOUR ("People need to get over it and get with it. This is how we now talk and text."), say,

"Innocent humor is one thing, but sarcasm, mocking, and meanness toward anyone stains your reputation and ruptures relationships. Manners still matter."

- TO THE ANTI-SOCIAL ("I want to be left alone, so I push people away. I don't want to be bothered."), say,

  "If you seek autonomy, don't push people away with rudeness. Politely say, 'I need to be alone. Thanks for understanding. You are kind.' They'll respond so much better."

- TO THE DEAF ("I think others are hearing things; I don't hear unkindness in my voice at all."), say,

  "Are people asking whether you are mad, if you love them, or why you are unkind? If you look and sound unkind, people have a legitimate right to think you are. Listen to how you sound."

- TO THE OFFSPRINGER ("People need to chill out. This is how my family of origin reacts in conflict."), say,

  "You inherited from your parents a style of conflict resolution that entails angrily screaming at each other. I get it, but I do not respond well at all when you yell at me."

- TO THE ABUSER ("I'm not abusive, and whatever idiot says that better guard his back."), say,

  "When a person denies being abusive, then reacts

in an abusive way, he proves the accusation. It's like a drunk slurring, 'My blood alcohol count is wrong.'"

- TO THE SELF-HATER ("Stressed out, under-exercised, and overeating, I react. I don't like myself."), say,

  "I ask, 'Why so mean today?' You reply, 'I don't like myself. I feel fat and stressed out.' I'm sorry you don't like yourself, but I care about you, and it doesn't help when you push me away with your attitude."

In Conclusion

Unfortunately, it is simply not the way of the world to always speak kindly and respectfully to others. Every day we see politicians tweeting rudely about their opponents, friends lambasting their bosses on Facebook, or sports fans getting into heated discussions about the coaches and players who have "ruined their life" with their latest decisions and play on the field. In all honesty, we sometimes feel as they feel. But we would be wise to remember the words of the apostle Paul, who himself dealt often with Jews, Romans, even Christians who found themselves ranging from simply disagreeing with his decisions to wanting to imprison and kill him. He wrote, "Let your speech *always* be with grace, as though seasoned with salt" (Col. 4:6).

Always. With grace.

Not only when someone agrees with you. Not only when he or she is kind first. Not only when you have something to gain from being kind. But always.

It isn't about the other person. It is about me, independent of the other person.

CHAPTER 3

IS IT NECESSARY?

Scriptural Meditation on Necessary Speech

- Ecclesiastes 3:7—**A time to be silent and a time to speak.**
- Proverbs 10:19—When there are **many words,** transgression is unavoidable, but he who restrains his lips is wise.
- Ecclesiastes 5:3—**Many words** mark the speech of a fool (NIV).
- Ecclesiastes 6:11—**The more the words, the less the meaning,** and how does that profit anyone? (NIV)
- Proverbs 29:20—Do you see a man who is **hasty in his words?** There is more hope for a fool than for him.

- Ecclesiastes 5:7—For in . . . **many words there is emptiness.**
- Ecclesiastes 10:12-14—The lips of a fool consume him; the beginning of his talking is folly and the end of it is wicked madness. Yet **the fool multiplies words.**
- Matthew 12:36—But I tell you that **every careless word** that people speak, they shall give an accounting for it in the day of judgment.
- James 1:26—If anyone thinks himself to be religious, and yet does not **bridle his tongue** but deceives his own heart, this man's religion is worthless.
- Ephesians 5:4—And there must be no filthiness and silly talk, or coarse jesting, **which are not fitting,** but rather giving of thanks.
- Ephesians 4:29—Let no unwholesome word proceed from your mouth, but only such a word as is good for edification **according to the need of the moment,** so that it will give grace to those who hear.
- Proverbs 25:11-12—Like apples of gold in settings of silver is a word **spoken in right circumstances.** Like an earring of gold and an ornament of fine gold is a wise reprover to a listening ear.
- Proverbs 15:23—A man has joy in **an apt answer,** and how delightful is **a timely word!**
- Proverbs 17:27—He who **restrains his words** has

knowledge, and he who has a cool spirit is a man of understanding.

- Proverbs 13:3—The one who **guards his mouth** preserves his life; the one who opens wide his lips comes to ruin.
- Proverbs 21:23—He who **guards his mouth and his tongue**, guards his soul from troubles.
- Proverbs 17:28—Even a fool, when he **keeps silent**, is considered wise; when he **closes his lips**, he is considered prudent.
- James 1:19—This you know, my beloved brethren. But everyone must be quick to hear, **slow to speak** and slow to anger.
- Jude 1:3—I felt the **necessity to write**.
- Ephesians 5:12—For it is **disgraceful even to speak** of the things which are done by them in secret.

A Quick Checklist to Get Us Started

Should we say something or refrain from commenting? Well, Ecclesiastes 3:7 reminds us that there is "a time to be silent and a time to speak." In other words, we must determine if this is a moment to stay quiet or speak what's on our hearts and minds.

The apostle Paul gives us a clue when he wrote, "Let no unwholesome word proceed from your mouth, but only such a word as is good for edification *according to the need of the moment*, so that it will give grace to those who hear" (Eph. 4:29). In other words, when the other person needs to hear it, and we can convey it in a wholesome and uplifting way, then it is necessary to communicate.

Before we get into the heart of communicating what is necessary, let's begin with a quick checklist to help us answer if it is necessary.

- If untrue, unkind, or unclear, then *no*, I will not communicate it. When is it ever necessary to say something that is a lie, mean, and confusing?
- If the other person needs to hear the truth, and I can communicate it kindly and clearly, then *yes*, I will communicate it. Because I care about the truth and because I care for the other person, I will courageously and kindly speak up in a way he or she understands. I will not remain silent. Though this book warns against speaking before thinking, the other side of this book asserts that when we conclude the other person needs the light of the truth, and we can speak it lovingly, respectfully, and coherently, then we ought to communicate it. We must speak up for

the sake of the truth and for the sake of the other person.

- If *yes*, but it is not the right time, I will *wait*. For instance, we may need to wait because the other person is not ready to hear from us today because he or she has been up all night and needs to rest. Or we need to wait until we can communicate face-to-face instead of over the phone. A basic rule is when in doubt wait twenty-four hours. When upset and feeling like you are not your normal self, sit on saying anything in writing for at least a day.

The Heart of Communicating What Is Necessary

As we have quoted, Jesus said in Matthew 12:34, "For the mouth speaks out of that which fills the heart." And Jesus went on to say in verses 36–37, "But I tell you that every careless word that people speak, they shall give an accounting for it in the day of judgment. For by your words you will be justified, and by your words you will be condemned." Careless words come out of an uncaring heart.

A person who modeled thinking before speaking what was unnecessary was my mom. My parents divorced when I was one, remarried, then separated again for five years. Even though Mom could've thrown Dad under the bus while raising me on her own, I appreciate that she abstained from doing so. She expressed later in her life that it was unnecessary for me to hear such things. Mom was other-focused. Because of her heart of love for me, she sought to serve my needs with her words. She was not careless in her words because she cared. She pulled back from communicating information that I didn't need to hear, even though she may have felt better after having done it.

As I have reflected on my mom, who is in heaven now, I do not recall my mom doing any of the following. She had a sense about what was necessary and what wasn't. She wasn't perfect, but she was mature.

Toward me, she did not

- provide too much information that overwhelmed me and caused me to tune her out,
- explode in anger and spew out hollow threats,
- make truthful comments at the wrong time that caught me off guard or cornered me,
- keep asking questions about things she knew would invade my privacy,

- keep on rehashing something that upset her,
- feel sorry for herself and look to me or anyone to hear her complaints,
- think she could say anything, anytime because she cared, and caring excused imprudence,
- dislike silence to the extent that she filled the room with her empty chatter to hear herself,
- overstate and exaggerate,
- interrupt because what she had to say trumped anything I had to say,
- grumble about unmet pleasures, or
- keep thinking of one more criticism to pile on.

I thank God that my mom worked at saying only what was necessary. She did this because she had a good and discerning heart.

The Golden Rule of Necessary Communication

How does the Golden Rule apply to unnecessary words?

Since we do not enjoy people who exhaustingly talk on and on, tell things about us to others who have no right to know, rehash the same episode about us without ever forgiving and forgetting, feel a compulsive obsession to fill in the silence with the sound of their voices, and keep dumping judgmental information on us that floods us emotionally, then why would we dare speak this way to others?

Since we do not enjoy people who explode with anger to make themselves feel better and attempt to change us, bellyache about their unfulfilled carnal dreams, grab the attention in conversations because they find us boring, and spew out their inflated woes to anyone lending half an ear, then why would we communicate this way?

Since we do not enjoy people who constantly police our activities to catch us, confront, and control our mistakes; ask too many questions that invade our privacy and feed their selfish curiosity to know; sidestep our honest questions to evade addressing what is the essential issue; and bring up stuff that is unfitting and distasteful; then why would we do such things?

Since we do not enjoy people who have an uncanny ability to habitually say the right thing at the wrong time, start talking before they have grasped the real concern on our hearts, mouth motherly platitudes that make us feel like toddlers, interrupt us when we are thoughtfully engaged with another person, and feel a divine call to lecture us like a bald-headed man selling hair restoration oil, then why would we express ourselves this way?

Why Do We Communicate What Is Unnecessary?

There are twenty descriptions that help us discern the reasons we have crossed the line and relayed unneeded and, many times, unwanted information. Please consider if any of these depict you, and then read the brief commentary on that profile about unnecessary speech.

If others softly rebuke us with, "What you're saying and doing isn't necessary," which of the following reasons may have prompted their remark? In other words, what rationalization do you have in your mind for communicating this way?

THE TMI PERSON: I think I provide helpful information, but some feel overwhelmed, so they say.

THE VOLCANO: I have to vent my pent-up feelings; it isn't healthy to repress my negativity.

THE COARSE: Admittedly, my words are off-color, but others shouldn't be such prudes.

THE UNTIMELY: What I said was true; it doesn't matter if that was the wrong time and place.

THE GOSSIP: I must be the first to know and tell, though, I suppose, some of it isn't my business.

THE PRYING: Not knowing the details, I have to meddle to enable me to advance my cause.

THE LOOSE CANNON: Yes, I unthinkingly mouth unwarranted stuff, but there's no ill will.

THE NON-LISTENER: Admittedly, I listen with half an ear until I can say what I want to say.

THE REHASHER: I've got to go over it again. I can't drop it and move on until I feel okay.

THE PITY-PARTIER: I have sorrows, okay? I look for anyone who will listen to my burdens.

THE SPY: I don't see it as snooping but as monitoring their mistakes to help them improve.

THE MOTHER: When others aren't listening to me, I say it anyway because I care.

THE CHATTERBOX: I dislike silence, so I fill it with whatever I am thinking at the time.

THE EXAGGERATOR: Honestly, to ignite empathy and change, I jarringly overstate reality.

THE INTERRUPTER: Folks tell me I interrupt them unnecessarily, but what I say is important.

THE GRUMBLER: When I don't get what I want, I'm unhappy and feel it's my right to gripe.

THE DISTRACTOR: I refuse to be put on the hot seat, so I sidetrack others with unrelated stuff.

THE LIMELIGHTER: Other people are quiet or boring, so I take center stage with my interests.

THE PILE-ON-ER: When upset, I think of additional
stuff and say it; it's not off topic to me.
THE UNPRAYERFUL: Maybe I should wait quietly in
prayer, but I feel they need to hear it now.

The TMI Person

Over the years I have received hundreds of e-mails
from spouses who dump the truck of information. They
tell me that they have a bad marriage, but then they tell me
about their mothers' health, the landlord's unresponsive-
ness, the dog running away, the mechanic overcharging,
the doctor not seeing them for three more months, putting on extra weight, needing a better health plan, and so
on. Though I know their hearts are in the right place, I
stop reading. I cannot absorb all the unnecessary information. It is classic TMI—too much information.

The TMI person is usually smart but overly insecure.
The insecurity drives him or her to get the other person to
fully understand. For this reason, the TMI person needs
to ask, "How much information is necessary to make my
point?" And when not knowing, give a little information
and ask if the other person needs more. The best thing for
the TMI person is to remember that less is more.

Others are not insecure but still give too much information. At board meetings at the organizations I led, I
would sometimes over-prepare on a proposal and present

way too much information. My desire for the board members to see my reasoning and position for the purpose of debate would eventually backfire because the avalanche of information became too much for them to absorb all at once.

Here's a clue if we are a TMI. When we talk, do we notice people looking at their watches or iPhones? Do we hear people saying, "Good, that's enough. I get it. Thanks"? Do people get up and leave the room when we talk? Does the boss say, "Just begin with a one-page summary, and if we want more, we'll ask"?

One person wrote me who had an awakening to TMI and made a commitment to reform. He said, "My new unspoken motto to strive to live by: K.I.S.S. (Keep It Simple Stupid)." Maybe a better slogan is "Keep It Short, Stupid." This is not bad advice for the TMI person to think about before hitting send.

The Volcano

Volcano eruptions happen over the phone with a family member accusing us of not caring and even lying, when replying to an e-mail from someone who just did an end run around our authority, with a coworker who criticizes our work again, or when tweeting about a candidate we can't stand. When upset, some of us let it fly like hot molten lava.

I have known of men with serious anger problems who explode at those around them, but afterward they feel great and expect those burnt to a crisp to say, "Hey, no problem. We fully understand."

When we become Volcanoes, most close off to us and may resent us. We hear them saying, "I have to walk on eggshells around this person." They see us as unpredictable, emotional, and irrational when hurt, frustrated, confused, angry, fearful, or offended. If they employ us, eventually they unemploy us. In social media, people skip over what we have written because the lava overrides the point.

Can we change? Absolutely. One woman wrote to me after she recognized her Volcano tendencies. She said, "Now, I am aware enough to stop and think when I feel myself wanting to say things out of my frustration. I don't shoot my mouth off. I think about how I come across."

This mind-set comes in handy just before hitting send!

The Coarse

I have found it strange that good and decent individuals for some unknown reason feel that they will be more popular if they can get people to laugh at their off-color comments or crude silliness. Sadly, their coarse jesting contributes nothing to the discussion other than the fact that they are trying to be funny. Most who listen find it in poor taste.

Mere silliness can be a problem. I know of one individual who lost his job because he would not stop his silly talk, like imitating actors and saying lines from sitcoms. He was never dirty, just imbecilic. He received several formal warnings from his superiors that such frivolity was conduct unbecoming his professional position, and they instructed him to stop. He did not heed their counsel, and they released him of his duties. Sadly, he was a Christian who knew this scripture: "There must be no filthiness and silly talk, or coarse jesting, which are not fitting, but rather giving of thanks" (Eph. 5:4).

Pray tell, why do some folks continue when it isn't needful? And worse, why do they claim others are prudes when all the facts show them as lacking prudence? This seems to be par for the Coarse.

The Untimely

What do I mean when I say something is true but unnecessary to say at this time? Parents know. If a daughter is overeating, it is true that she needs instruction on why she should cut back on desserts. However, the parents don't give her that information in front of her brothers. One of the brothers is apt to tease or blurt out unkind comments. At that moment those words, because of the parents' untimely instruction, are etched on the soul of that daughter for the next seventy years. There is a time and place to communicate information.

A husband, who works in an office, took time off to physically labor twelve hours to help a friend move. He's exhausted. At the same time, his wife had an altercation with their teen son and feels overwhelmed. She feels like a complete failure and can hardly wait for her husband to return home so they can talk. As he enters the door, she launches into explaining what happened with their son. But a few minutes into her report the husband says, "I am sorry, honey. Can we talk about this in the morning?" She reacts, "No, I need to talk now. This is tearing me apart."

Technically she is not wrong about needing to talk, but neither is he in knowing he is falling asleep. His exhaustion trumps her need to talk at that hour. We need to recognize that true information communicated at the wrong time usually proves useless.

Are you about to hit send on some communication that you are not sure if now is the right time to send it? Yes, it is true, and it may be kind, but will it arrive at such a bad time that the truth and kindness will fall on deaf ears because it feels as though you have forced yourself on this person and situation? As many of us have heard, timing is everything. If you are uncertain if this is the best time, wait on it. Put the e-mail in your drafts and come back to it when you have certainty about the timing. Right words at the wrong time don't feel right to the other person.

The Gossip

The Gossip says, "I have information you don't know. Look to me as the first to know and the first to tell. I have the inside scoop. I know others' business in order to tell their business."

Some gossip can turn malicious. In addressing the performance of an employee he does not like, the manager tells the CEO, "Well, you don't know this, but his boy is into drugs, and his wife is seeing another man." The CEO now wonders, *Does this manager have loose lips? Can I trust him with confidential information? If he tells me things that I should not know, will he tell others things about this business that they should not know?*

All of us have heard, "Some things are best left unsaid." To assist us in discerning what is best unsaid, a good rule of thumb is "Do not repeat any information you won't sign your name to." I have a pastor friend who carries around a 3x5 card, and when people begin to gossip, he starts taking notes on what they're saying and then tells them he's going to go to the person about whom they are talking to tell that person what's being said. Gossips stopped coming to him because they would not put their names to the gossip.

Another rule of thumb: be part of the solution, not

part of the problem. This pastor friend also tells the Gossip, "We are going to this person about whom you are talking to ask if this is true, and, if so, what we can do to help. We are going to be part of the solution here."

The Prying

A caring interest in the daily activities of others is good, but being too inquisitive is out of line since it is an invasion of privacy and can come from an unhealthy intrigue.

The problem is that some who pry don't see themselves as prying. They see themselves as caring. Sarah, my wife, talks about the twenty questions she would ask our son David every day after school when he was in the fifth grade. About a week into this regimen, David said, "Mom, it's the same every day. If anything changes, I'll let you know." Like every mother, Sarah wanted to connect with her son's heart. She cared. From her womanly vantage point, that could happen only through talking. But because David did not talk to Sarah as she longed for, she felt compelled to ask questions to draw him out. In my book *Mother & Son*, I address what a mom can do in this situation. But a mother must ask herself, *Is this prying or connecting? Will my son feel uncomfortable because it doesn't feel friendly but more like an investigation to find out information about him in order to criticize him?* At best, she must reassure him that is not her motive.

Some of us pry because we cannot stand not knowing. We may be Gossips, and this is how we uncover the unknown. Some of us push others beyond the boundaries with which they feel comfortable. We pry information from a church board member by peppering him with a hundred questions about who the board might hire as the worship leader, and we intend to use this information to garner support ahead of time to oppose the candidate if we do not like this worship leader. We pry information from a member of the management team on the compensation package so as to create a firestorm of resistance given the package is less than requested. Whenever strife is in the air on issues that matter to us (Prov. 26:17), we feel compelled to meddle. We snoop for the scoop to advance our interests. For example, we send off an e-mail with questions that we cloak in innocent-sounding ways, but we are prying open the lid on information that we intend to use for our selfish agenda. We create trouble with the data with the hope we get what we want. The Bible refers to us as "a troublesome meddler" (1 Peter 4:15). This type of person is not conducting himself in an above-board manner but has improperly crossed the line into a covert operation. It is necessary to debate not deceive.

Before hitting send (thinking metaphorically) ask this question: Why am I asking so many questions?

Is prying connected with your "fear of missing out"?

Tiffany Bloodworth Rivers says, "Because we *can* be so connected, many feel that they *have to be* connected at all times. In fact, there is a real psychological condition, fear of missing out (or FOMO), which is growing amongst members of our society, in which people feel a compulsion to know what is happening, communicate with, or share information with any and all people, places, and things."[1] This feeds the prying proclivity.

Do you pry? Let me ask: If a neighbor dug a hole in the backyard late at night, would this drive you nuts until you knew why?

The Loose Cannon

In a board meeting of twelve people on Monday at the ABC Printing Company, Patti shares, "Cindy isn't at work today. She's taking a vacation day because she found out on Friday night that her husband is having an affair with his secretary."

That information is true, clear, and spoken out of empathy and kindness toward Cindy, who is Patti's good friend. However, that information is unnecessary. Not only does that information have nothing to do with the business of that meeting, it is none of those folks' business. Sadly, this becomes fuel for gossip, discredits her husband, who could be repenting at that very moment, and puts Cindy in jeopardy for a promotion she was up for.

Later in the year, Patti wonders why she doesn't get outside assignments. Someone tells her, "Management can't trust you with inside information! They view you as a loose cannon."

In battle or a storm, when a cannon breaks loose from its moorings, it does severe damage to ship and crew. It is uncontrolled and unpredictable.

Such a person defends, "I am not trying to hurt anybody. I am just being honest or expressing concern. I can't always help myself." But a lack of tongue-control is a sign of lack of self-control. The Bible refers to this as an unbridled tongue (James 1:26). The tongue is unrestrained like the unhinged flapping sail that suddenly snaps back and slaps you across the face. When a person does not control his lips, people get hurt.

Just because you are full of goodwill does not mean you should hit send. Good intentions do not always produce good words or outcomes. What comes out of the mouth isn't always the same as that which is in the heart. Goodwill and good sense are not synonymous. As the expression goes, "Loose lips sink ships."

The Non-Listener

Six-year-old Johnny asked his mother where he came from. She had prepared for this moment and went into a full explanation of human sexuality and the birth of a child. After she finished she asked him if she answered the question. Johnny said, "Maybe. Jason down the street just moved here, and he told me that he came from New York. I wanted to know where I came from."

We can miss what is being said. The other day I was talking to a husband who sat and listened to his adult son share his heart with his mother. For whatever reason, she was extremely defensive. She was so defensive that she went off on topics that were tangential to the issue being addressed by her son. At one point the husband said, "Honey, I don't think you're hearing what he is trying to say. Here is what he's feeling in his heart," to which his son totally agreed. The dad said to me, "I was amazed that she had no idea the extent to which she was missing his heart. I think she felt accused, since the conversation got off on the wrong foot with him yelling at her, and she felt he intended to condemn her as a bad mother. She filtered everything through that grid. She sat there fearful of what she might hear and thus didn't hear."

Proverbs 18:13 says, "He who gives an answer before he hears, it is folly and shame to him." Any one of us can end up missing the deeper issue. We tweet back a nasty comment only to realize we misunderstood, and now we have to apologize. All around the world people are forced to apologize because they were presumptuous. It seems we have become the apologetic country.

I am stunned when people make comments on social media platforms in response to some point that a person has supposedly made; but when one reads what the first person wrote, the reply completely misses what is communicated. In fact, others jump in and give their opinions. A thread of replies piles up that has nothing to do with the original point or questions. All of the commentary is unnecessary. Finally, a person chimes in, "Everyone is missing the point here."

We should make it our goal to echo this person, "I used to listen in order to speak, but now I find myself listening to understand."

Did you know the letters in the word *listen* are the same as in the word *silent*?

Before hitting send, ask yourself, *Have I listened carefully and understood the exact issue on the table?*

The Rehasher

A guy told me once, "She began . . . rehashing years of things that I did wrong, making me feel like I was stupid." A woman also told me, "He spends all of our time rehashing everything I ever did wrong."

In many cases, the rehasher is feeling insecure more than trying to condemn the other. One woman recognized this in herself. She needed to talk to resolve things. Unless she talked things through, she didn't feel right or secure and kept rehearsing in her mind and rehashing with others. But people were shutting down on her. She turned to her dad for advice. He said, "Honey, the question you need to ask is this, 'Will I remember this in a day, a week, a month, or a year from now. Will they?' If not, it is okay to let it go. That doesn't mean you shouldn't talk it through with the other person, but it may not be necessary." She told me this liberated her since no one had ever said that to her. All her life, she had felt everything was necessary to talk through whenever she felt bothered.

When I counsel couples, I share that certain chemicals in a woman cause her to stew for a twelve-hour period after a conflict. She rehearses the whole episode, finding it impossible to shake it. Whereas a man's chemical makeup differs, and he can stop stewing after one hour. This is why when a couple have a fight in the morning, that evening she needs to talk about what happened nine hours earlier, whereas he replies, "What are you talking about?" He honestly can't remember why she's upset. He has thought about a hundred things at work, and their flare-up earlier that morning is now in his rearview mirror. Two mature people need to decide whether to drop it, as he has, or talk about it because she still has a need to talk about it. Neither is wrong, just different.

Some things need to be overlooked, not written on a ledger to rehash every day until we feel secure as a person.

Love "keeps no record of wrongs" (1 Cor. 13:5 NIV), especially when the other person has understood that he or she came across poorly and apologized. We need to forgive and move on. It is not okay to beat a dead horse. Rehashing can shame the other, who now complains, "Is this necessary, again? What else can I say or do?"

Some of us need to give these matters to God, as Peter wrote, "casting all your anxiety on Him, because He cares for you" (1 Peter 5:7). A person wrote, "I still have times of weakness when I doubt (their) intentions. I seem to have a hard time stopping myself from thinking in the past and rehashing those feelings. I've been relying on prayer to help me through those issues."

Jesus said, "Come to Me, all who are weary and heavy-laden, and I will give you rest" (Matt. 11:28). Sounds like a great avenue to take! Before hitting send, maybe you should hit your knees.

The Pity-Partier

Over the years I have noticed some individuals hop from counselor to counselor. These individuals have no intention of changing. They simply want to tell their stories of woe to gain empathy. They derive energy from people who feel sorry for them. However, if a counselor shifts focus to what the person could change, he or she usually finds another counselor. Some people have an addiction to therapy, as opposed to needing therapy for an addiction.

Counselor-hoppers do the same at work. They have someone cornered at the drinking fountain, dumping out melancholy melodramas. Two days later they're at lunch with a different coworker, doing the same thing. They are not seeking help but feeling sorry for themselves, and persuading the listener to feel sorry for them. Actually, they are having a pity-party and inviting anyone who will show up.

For this reason, people love Facebook. How many tearfully post their stories with the hope that half a dozen people will affirm everything they are feeling? That no one knows the backstory, other than what they say, is such a convenience. Facebook does not demand two or three witnesses to confirm the facts of what they report. However, Moses, Jesus, and Paul do make that kind of demand (Deut. 19:15; Matt. 18:16; 2 Cor. 13:1).

For several years we unofficially tracked the number of people who e-mailed me to tell their stories of woe, but when we made several recommendations on what they could do, we never heard from them again. Before you hit send, may I ask a question? Why are you communicating this information? Are you having a pity party and want others to feel sorry for you, or do you seek wisdom on how to climb out of the pit?

The Spy

To spy is to secretly gather data on the activities of others without their consent. Unless we work for a governmental agency, it is unnecessary to spy. On a personal basis, we may have the best of intentions and seek only the truth. But the others don't know, and if they knew of our spying, it would undermine the trust in our relationships. It crosses the boundary into unwarranted territory. But more so, why are we spying? Most of us spy to catch others in wrongdoing.

Think of parents. There is no debate that parents must act responsibly toward their children and supervise them against wrongdoing. But some parents have confessed that they seek to be the Holy Spirit to their children. Because of their yearning to prevent their kids from encountering what they experienced at that age, they have an obsessive compulsion to track everything their teen is doing. The thought is, "If I catch them doing something wrong, this will motivate them to do what is right when I am not watching." These moms and dads spy to confront and correct, and yes, control.

By the way, there's no problem with accountability when the child knows up front about the monitoring. For instance, putting protective software on the computer is a good thing. Dad himself has this accountability. What *is* wrong is spying on the teen boy who talks to a girl in the park. That's undisclosed monitoring and will break trust in the event he finds out.

For the believer, this can be a crisis of faith. Sarah has told mothers of teenagers, "Tell the Lord, 'Lord, if there's anything I need to know, would You let me know?'" At some point we must trust God. We cannot spy 24/7.

Beyond parenting, some of us convince ourselves we spy or eavesdrop because we care. The stalker declares, "I am in love with her. All's fair in love and war." But beyond the creepy stalker, employers are spying on employees at epidemic rates because they "care" about the company. However, it is one thing to let the public and employee know "this phone call is recorded" but quite another to secretly spy via the technology available to monitor e-mails, Internet usage, GPS on a vehicle, etc. I take the position to let people know of the monitoring. There's no problem with accountability. What frightens and offends is when we do something behind their backs.

How do we know if we are spying? Are we doing surveillance and fear exposure? When we fear getting caught by those we seek to catch, we're a spy.

The Mother

It is one thing to be a mother who tells her son to be careful when he drives to school. Though she knows he isn't listening, she says it anyway. Perhaps she says it for fear something bad will happen to him and she does not wish to live in guilt for failing to give warning. Or perhaps she says "be careful" because she wants others to say that to her as a way of saying, "I am thinking about you because I have you on my heart."

However, there is another type of mothering that's inappropriate. At work, a female employee mothers a male peer by telling him to put on his jacket and comb his hair, or tells him to be careful driving home because the roads are slippery with ice. Though she isn't romantically interested in him by any stretch of the imagination, she has a special affection for him as a type of brother. (The roles can be reversed, and the man hovers over the woman.) However, she needs to discern if this is something he feels comfortable with. Unfortunately, she blinds herself to his unease with those maternal comments. Such a woman has so strong a need to be needed that she ignores the discomfort in this man's face and eyes. She does not ask herself, *Am I out of line? Are there boundaries here that I have no right or responsibility to cross? Am I seeking validation as a person?* She must not allow her need to care to trump her need to be discerning and prudent. Eventually, this male peer will tell her, "Look, I don't need you to mother me, okay? I appreciate that you're concerned, but you are here to do the tasks assigned to you by management. I don't need you to be my mother hen." In hearing this, she is stabbed in the heart and crushed. That evening she cries and cries from the pain she feels. However, she brought this on by "caring" where that type of care is not required at work. She may be a caring personality, but, like the rest of us, she must operate according to the code of behavior at work. She must not let her care override protocol or cross the boundaries that others have for themselves.

A wife may mother her husband unknowingly: "Tonight when we are with your mother, be nice to her. Talk to her. Ask her about her day. And when we have soup, don't slurp." She shames him as if he's ten years old, though she might believe it shows how much she cares. This husband blocked out his wife years ago. He doesn't listen. When this is pointed out, she replies, "Well, he acts like he's ten years old." And she wonders why he never romances her. Who wants to romance his mother?

Too, this caring mother figure can step over her boundaries by declaring others do not care. The classic example is Martha, the sister of Mary (Luke 10:38–42). When Jesus visited Martha's home, Martha was doing all the work preparing for the meal while her sister sat at the feet of Jesus. Martha said to Jesus, "Lord, do You not care that my sister has left me to do all the serving alone? Then tell her to help me." Note two things: She confronted the One who is perfect in love for not caring. Second, she commanded Him to get her sister to care. Caring people like Martha can be a bit self-righteous and bossy but not see it. May I suggest to you that she overreached with the Son of God?

Before hitting send, ask, *Am I about to mother someone beyond appropriate rules of engagement or wrongly judge another as uncaring?*

The Chatterbox

Some of us have nothing to say, but we talk anyway. That's not easy to do, but we pull it off.

For example, we are in the workroom of a company with five others, sorting and preparing documents for distribution, and we start chatting. At one level, we are being socially delightful, especially when we tell interesting stories. But chatterbox Betty talks about the new wastebasket in the ladies' room that reminds her that she needs to get a wastebasket for her freshly painted bathroom at home, which took three weeks to paint because she couldn't get the color correct. That then reminds her of her grandmother, who had only an outhouse but lived to ninety-two and died in the local hospital, which she learned just added a new wing for drug addicts. She is off and running, saying a lot about nothing, and, at a certain point, no one cares, and everyone stops listening.

The Chatterbox feels compelled to talk when nothing needs to be said. One person who identified herself as a Chatterbox said she was on the phone and suddenly became aware that she felt as if she had no control over what she was saying. She felt like she was on autopilot, going on and on. What amazed this person at a point of self-illumination was that she knew at the time that she was thinking of something else while her lips were moving on this topic. It frightened her that she had nothing to say but talked anyway, not even engaged in her own conversation. That takes talent.

The Chatterbox needs to ask himself or herself several questions:

- *Do I talk even though I don't need to say anything?*
- *Why do I feel I must be the one to talk when no one is talking?*
- *Upon reflection, do others listen when I talk?*
- *If not, is that because I drone on like white noise that puts others to sleep?*
- *Does it bother me when I'm interrupted and later no one asks me to resume what I was saying?*
- *Do I even care to resume what I was saying?*
- *Do I or anyone else even remember what I was saying?*

If the answers to these questions are unfavorable, one is talking unnecessarily.

The Exaggerator

I received an e-mail once from a person who wrote, **Last week he blurted out he wanted a divorce which he has said before but never acted upon.**

Why does the guy say he wants a divorce? He seeks to convey the depth of his pain in the relationship with her. He makes an outlandish remark with the underlying desire that she will hear his cry and change. Of course, it sounds like a threat or ultimatum for self-serving purposes to coerce her into doing what he wants. Instead of meeting his wife's need for love, he speaks unnecessary words to frighten her into doing what he deems necessary! Go figure.

In a moment of utter frustration over not being promoted, a female vice president exclaimed to her all-male management team, "I feel like all the men on this management team hate women. You deceive others into thinking that you care about women, but you don't. You give the impression to outsiders that there is no glass ceiling in this organization, but that's a crock." She didn't believe much of what she said, but she said it nonetheless. She expected them to decode the real meaning behind her words. However, when we say untrue, unkind, and unclear things—which, obviously, are totally unnecessary—there is a price to pay. This woman was removed from the management team.

Here's an e-mail from a woman who overstated her concern about her marriage:

> I told my sister, in confidence, I thought, that I wished I was dead or my husband was dead, so I could escape these circumstances. . . . She proceeded to call my daughter, who got worried. And my daughter called my husband. Well, of course, this was very hurtful and embarrassing to [my husband]. . . . [My husband] says I have just about killed all feeling he has for me.

Why did she say such things about wishing she were dead or her husband were dead? She wanted to ignite empathy from her sister, but it backfired because she never intended her jarring overstatements about reality to go beyond the private conversation with her sister.

Hurt, frustrated, angry, confused, fearful, or offended, we burst out with unnecessary injections. We do not mean it like it sounds. We're trying to bring about some change in the situation or relationship. We hope the others around us will decode our deepest meaning and possibly rescue us by apologizing and making things right. But it doesn't happen, not often. When we make inflammatory exclamations, such as "Go ahead and divorce me! I hate you! You never respected me!" we undermine the very aim we hold deep in our hearts: reconciliation and the experience of love and respect.

We cannot tell our parents they are the worst human beings on the planet as a way of motivating them to heal us emotionally. We cannot tell a boss it is pure hell to work for him and expect him to create a heavenly work environment for us.

At the moment, we may feel like we are truthfully describing our feelings, but when our passions are out of control, we will overstate reality. Such exaggeration will cause others to dismiss our deepest concerns because they will see us as out of line if not irrational. No matter how saintly our motive is in bringing about righteous changes, others will back away from us.

The Interrupter

Several wives have communicated to me their frustrations similar to the one expressed in this e-mail:

> He interrupts me when I try to speak; then I feel disrespected, unheard . . . I then react to him by raising my voice and telling him to listen to me. I try to continue, but he interrupts to tell me what I'm feeling or what he thinks I should do. I get even more offended.

All of this is unnecessary.

I have heard over the years that in business, men interrupt people far more than do women. Women will go quiet out of deference to the other. Generally speaking, they exercise a greater sensitivity. At the same time, in the home most wives criticize and complain, so husbands withdraw and stonewall when things get heated up, which prompts the wives to come at them to talk, no matter what their husbands are now doing at the moment.

Regardless of our gender and setting, all of us must recognize that when we think that what we want to say is the most important thing that needs to be said, we are tempted to interrupt.

For instance, two people are discussing a project in the conference room, and an individual enters to tell them that he just got tickets to an NFL game. That's nice information, but it's irrelevant to their discussion and interrupts their flow of thought. Furthermore, his real point in interrupting is to brag that the boss just gave him the tickets.

Some interruptions are innocent but annoying nonetheless. My daughter Joy e-mailed me to say,

I usually stumble upon the last few episodes of the Bachelor/ette with friends who are very engrossed in

the TV program. But they get annoyed as I interrupt
constantly about the editing and acting, not to
mention the cries of, "Are you kidding me!?"

"But, Emerson, what about the work arena? I am in
charge. These people are under me. I have the authority here and should be able to speak my thoughts at any
time." To this argument, I would say that the most effective leaders are not authoritarian. They are strong but
gracious in asking, "Would this be a good time to describe
a situation to you, or would later be better?" Most folks
will immediately defer to the leader and will be appreciative of the sensitivity. People know that a leader has the
greater responsibility and with that come certain rights,
one of which is the right to interrupt. However, he need
not be rude. He can say, "Sorry to interrupt, but I have a
couple of important items to cover that just came to my
attention. Again, I apologize to take you from what you
are doing, so thank you for allowing me to do this."

It comes back to the Golden Rule. Just do what we
would want done to us.

The Grumbler

As a high school senior at a military school, I had the
good fortune of receiving several meaningful awards at
graduation. However, I did not receive one award that

I wanted and shared my disappointment with a fellow cadet. I still remember his shock and look of complete disbelief, and his words, "Your fellow classmates just voted you most likely to succeed, and that's not good enough. You still want more." He said it respectfully as my friend, but I could see an element of disbelief in him that I would say something that was so self-focused and unappreciative.

At that moment, as an eighteen-year-old, I embarrassingly recognized something repellent in me. I was grumbling about not getting one more pleasure. I wanted, so to speak, fifteen Christmas presents, not twelve. To him, my comments were uncalled for. To this day, more than forty years later, I still recall the shame I felt over making that ungrateful comment. It was not an acceptable remark but a complaint rooted in my carnal self-love, and I did not see it until he confronted me on my pettiness.

Grumbling about what we don't have is the offspring of conceit. We feel that we deserve more than we already have. We go through life saying, "I deserve that, not them!" It all sounds so trivial, except to ourselves.

So much of what we complain about when interacting with others is unnecessary since it is based on us wanting more of what we already have. We end up being like the person who said, "I whined about not having a third pair of shoes until I saw a man with no feet." Truth is, much of our lives is golden, but we call it jaundiced.

As a Christian, when I bellyache about not getting what I deserve (or think I deserve), I need to pause and remember there is another side to what I deserve. Truth is, I deserve God's judgment for all my transgressions but am not receiving this judgment because of His grace and mercy extended to me though Jesus Christ. That should stop some of my grousing and saying stupid, trifling, and unnecessary stuff about how bad I have it. Truth is, it could be worse and should be. And the additional truth is, I have it better than it should be.

The Distractor

When a four-year-old asks us how babies are made, we distract them by saying, "Hey, look at the bird in that tree. What kind of bird is that? Let's look in our bird book, and then let's make cookies." That kind of distraction is appropriate and necessary.

There are other distractions that are less appropriate. For instance, judges and lawyers do not allow information that is irrelevant or beyond the scope of the case. They especially disfavor uncalled-for remarks that are inflammatory and cause prejudice (pre-judging). Furthermore, judges and lawyers do not allow witnesses to ramble on about nothing in order to avoid telling the truth. This is why in the court the judge demands, "Please answer the question, no more and no less."

Another arena in which we observe a person refusing to be put on the hot seat is when a politician is interviewed. The politician skirts around the issue, refusing to answer the question. That can be a good thing or a tactic to avoid unpopular information. In fact, did you know there is an art to distraction that most politicians know to employ? When questioned, ask a question in return, attack the question, attack the questioner, plead ignorance, or jump to another topic.

When we are being a Distractor, we are not untruthful per se, but we are trying to keep away from subjects we prefer not to address. That can be a wise thing, or it can be interpreted by others as our unwillingness to address an important topic that is necessary for them to gather information about. We talk about the unnecessary to avoid the necessary.

The Limelighter

Returning from summer vacation, a female professor saw another professor in the hall and asked, "So, Jason, how was your summer?" Jason launched into a thirty-minute description of all he did during summer vacation, entertaining Susan with his numerous stories to which she laughed. When Jason finished, he looked at his watch and said he had to go, to which Susan replied, "Well, Jason, it would have been nice for you to ask how my summer went." With a twinkle in his eyes Jason replied, "Frankly, Susan, I don't care."

Storytellers grab center stage. Some are quite entertaining. I have a hilarious friend who tells the same stories in social settings, but everyone, along with me, loves to hear the same episodes again and again. In fact, her friends hold up fingers to show how many times they've heard this particular episode, but they let her continue because she has them crying again with laughter. But few have this endearing ability. Almost every Limelighter is egotistical, wishing only to hear his own voice since he views others as relatively unimportant. We observe this with ego-driven intellectuals or extroverts who talk on and on about what they prize. As people say, "They like listening to themselves."

I came across this person's words. They capture the pain of being in the shadows when the Limelighter shows up:

Once or twice a week I find myself having lunch with coworkers, or dinner with friends of friends, at which there is someone who just won't shut up, or who talks too loud, or who has little to say but takes forever to say it, or who always talks about the same topics. It's exhausting, and frustrating for others who wouldn't mind chiming in with their own thoughts every now and again. Why do they do this and what's the best way to handle them? I'm a quiet person. I enjoy a good chat, but I like it to be mellow and relaxed, and always make an effort to bring other people in where I can. Some people just completely lack this social skill. They think they are fun and that their energy livens things up, when actually they are stopping other people from enjoying themselves.[2]

Are you a Limelighter? Is this how you wish to be as a person? I don't think so. You need to get the spotlight off yourself and put that light on those around you. They will love and respect you so much more as you show your continued interest in their lives.

The Pile-On-er

I have a friend who, when he gets going on things that bother him, will humorously exclaim, in imitation of what others say, "And one more thing!" I laugh because we know this is what people do in heated conversations.

This add-on sentence keeps the fight going. For example, a woman criticizes her husband for failing to remember to pick up her clothing at the cleaners and uses this to drive home the point that he doesn't care. But she piles on. "And one more thing, you care about your mother more than you care about me. You call her a couple of times a week but never call me like that. And another thing, you mismanage money like your mother mismanages money. Like mother, like son."

It is too much. He feels punched and pummeled. He shuts down, and then she uses that as one more thing to prove that he doesn't care because he refuses to talk to her about her feelings.

Piling it on this way is comparable to piling eight thirty-pound stones on his head until he feels like his neck is breaking. It is too much of a burden. He can't handle it.

People who realized their tendencies to be Pile-On-ers have shared with me that they pile on stuff in an argument that has been disturbing them about the other person, even though it has nothing to do with the issue on the table. They also admit that they oftentimes speak what is unnecessary because they do not believe speaking only what is necessary is enough. And many have shared that they never realized how their constant criticisms were affecting the other.

And one more thing, are you guilty of always saying, "And one more thing"?

The Unprayerful

Within the church community we often hear people readily confess that they can get preachy with people in their world, whether in the home or at work. Though they do not stand on a street corner with tambourine and Bible, they relay their sense that they should be more prayerful and patient.

When we are too preachy, the listener tunes us out. A person confessed that he used preachy, pushy, nagging, and complaining words that turned the other person off. He recognized it was all unnecessary and triggered resentment in the other person.

Though Paul asks in the book of Romans, how will they hear unless a preacher is sent (Rom. 10:14), Peter also instructs certain people to refrain from using words when those words are not getting through (1 Peter 3:1–2). Many of us have heard "preach the gospel, and if necessary use words."

Take a look at what a few people wrote to me:

- I have come to the conclusion that maybe this is one of those times that God is telling me to keep my mouth shut and just continue to pray.
- I decided to keep my mouth shut (for the first time in a while), listen, read, and let God show me.
- I continued to pray and kept my mouth shut! Guess what happened . . . I believe God provided us a miracle because I chose to control my tongue and my attitude.

We need to allow God to be God in the other person's life. As the T-shirt says, "He's God, You're Not." Before hitting send, we should ask ourselves if this communication will feel to others as if we are hitting their sins. Do we need to delete this communication for the time being and instead pray and serve them?

Why Should We Communicate What Is Necessary?

The other person needs to hear what is necessary. In our ten-session Love and Respect Marriage Mentoring of Couples in Crisis, we provide couples, after about five sessions, an evaluation form that we refer to as the Core Issues of the Heart. There are seven of them: lack of self-control, unforgiveness, selfishness, pride, deceit, laziness, and lack of faith.

As the trust relationship deepens between the mentoring couple and the couple in crisis, we ask the crisis couple to answer several key questions about their own hearts. This is a self-report. We do this because usually one of the seven issues sabotages any movement forward as a husband and wife. After they turn in their self-report, based on a series of phrases that might identify them, one of these seven usually surfaces since their answers provide a cluster of similar responses. Then we highlight from their own critique the area they need to face. We have realized that if we don't take steps in pointing out what is necessary for them to see about themselves, they will have a tough time moving forward. Because we care, we convey what is necessary for them to hear from their own self-assessment. The amazing thing is that most people are very appreciative when they know that these things are shared out of a burden for them and from a desire for them to experience their best selves.

Does this mean everyone responds positively? No. For instance, over the years I have tried to affirm Christians to trust Christ and follow His will for their lives. I try to honor them with a noble vision to remain true to the God they love and who loves them. I do not preach but share. However, after hearing my challenge, some carnal Christians go their own way. I never hear from them again. Even so, I know that my silence can deprive them of their need to move forward as God intends. If I remained silent, I would restrict their options. I see myself providing them with a right of refusal. I afford them the opportunity to hear the good news of God's ultimate, loving plan for them.

Winston Churchill said, "Criticism may not be agreeable, but it is necessary. It fulfills the same function as pain in the human body; it calls attention to the development of an unhealthy state of things."[3]

You need to ask yourself, *When the people with whom I associate need to hear the necessary truth kindly and clearly spoken, will I tell them?* Silence is not always golden.

We must show ourselves that we have the courage to do so. My wife and I, along with millions of others, enjoyed the movie *The Help*. The movie, which is set in Jackson, Mississippi, in the 1960s, captures the oppressive experiences of black women who served in the homes of whites as "the help." In fact, these wonderful black women raised the children of the whites.

One such white daughter, Skeeter, was raised by Constantine, a black woman, and finds out after she goes off to college that her mother, Charlotte, fired Constantine, who faithfully worked more than thirty years for the family. The firing happened because a group of white women, certain dignitaries, were eating at Charlotte's home when Constantine's daughter arrived home from college and came through the front door, which she had done from childhood. One of the women confronted Charlotte over this outrageous behavior because blacks were to use the back door. This woman demanded that Charlotte act. Instead of courageously standing up for Constantine, Charlotte gave in to the racism of the culture and fired Constantine.

Later Charlotte confesses to Skeeter her horrible cowardice and says, "Courage sometimes skips a generation."

She praises Skeeter for having the courage to speak the necessary truth in her book *The Help*, which exposed the arrogant injustice toward these faithful black women.

Do we need to hit send? Yes, it is very necessary when those around us communicate what is intentionally untrue, unkind, unnecessary, and unclear. We have a moral obligation. We must

- correct their intentional lies with what is true,
- kindly confront their intentional unkindnesses,
- point out that what they said was intentionally unnecessary, and
- be clear with them about where they were intentionally unclear.

I will give an account to God not only for what I said that was unnecessary but also for failing to say what was necessary. We have made the point that our heavenly Father loves us and is listening to our conversations. As He knows the number of hairs on our heads (Matt. 10:30), so He knows everything we carelessly communicate (Matt. 12:36). Because Jesus Christ says this is important, it is important. One of the greatest incentives for communicating what is necessary is that we know this is what the Lord calls us to do. We do this out of trust and obedience toward Him, out of love and reverence for Him.

How Can We Respond to Others Who Communicate What Is Unnecessary?

- TO THE TMI PERSON ("I think I provide helpful information, but some feel overwhelmed, so they say."), say,

    "I usually appreciate the information you give. But less is more when you go into detail and inundate me with data that overloads me and ends in me tuning you out."

- TO THE VOLCANO ("I have to vent my pent-up feelings; it isn't healthy to repress my negativity."), say,

    "I've no problem with you sharing honest feelings. You have goodwill. But when you erupt to cool off at my expense, your words feel like hot molten lava."

- TO THE COARSE ("Admittedly, my words are off-color, but others shouldn't be such prudes."), say,

    "I have found many cool people who maintain a great reputation and significant influence but don't cross over into coarse jesting and silliness; it just isn't necessary."

- TO THE UNTIMELY ("What I said was true; it doesn't matter if that was the wrong time and place."), say,

    "What you told me was true, but I did not need

to receive the information at that time or in that place. Please think about when and where we are before you share with me."

- TO THE GOSSIP ("I must be the first to know and tell, though, I suppose, some of it isn't my business."), say,

    "You tell me things about others I shouldn't know. I'm not part of the problem or solution, nor are you. Let's stop, after you reassure me you're not talking about me like that."

- TO THE PRYING ("Not knowing the details, I have to meddle to enable me to advance my cause."), say,

    "A caring interest in the daily activities of others is good, but being too inquisitive is out of line since it is an invasion of privacy and says a lot about your unhealthy desire for intrigue."

- TO THE LOOSE CANNON ("Yes, I unthinkingly mouth unwarranted stuff, but there's no ill will."), say,

    "You have a good heart, but when we're with others, I'm not confident that you'll keep my confidences. You say private stuff others shouldn't know, and that hurts."

- TO THE NON-LISTENER ("Admittedly, I listen with half an ear until I can say what I want to say."), say,

    "I need you to hear my concerns, then talk. We

have two ears, one mouth; shouldn't we listen twice as much as we talk? I don't say this to hurt you but to convey my need to be heard."

- TO THE REHASHER ("I've got to go over it again. I can't drop it and move on until I feel okay."), say,

  "If others mistreat us, we don't have to rehash the incident. It's unnecessary and unhealthy. And when they seek our forgiveness and change their behaviors, rehashing it only reveals our insecurity, not their insincerity."

- TO THE PITY-PARTIER ("I have sorrows, okay? I look for anyone who will listen to my burdens."), say,

  "Feeling sorry for self is not always bad. Melancholy moments can recalibrate us. But you shouldn't stay at that party too long or invite other people to it. Your self-pity is excessive."

- TO THE SPY ("I don't see it as snooping but as monitoring their mistakes to help them improve."), say,

  "You cannot monitor a person 24/7, and even if you could, would you confront every questionable detail? It isn't necessary to police and report every act of another."

- TO THE MOTHER ("When others aren't listening to me, I say it anyway because I care."), say,

  "You speak up because you care. But you don't

discern when you've overstepped your boundaries; you don't have the right or responsibility to mother others."

- TO THE CHATTERBOX ("I dislike silence, so I fill it with whatever I am thinking at the time."), say,

     "Silence seems to bother you, and you chatter randomly. Some small talk is okay, but every moment doesn't have to be filled with words. Your silence also can give others opportunity to comment."

- TO THE EXAGGERATOR ("Honestly, to ignite empathy and change, I jarringly overstate reality."), say,

     "You blow your issue out of proportion, like when you claim, 'No one cares.' This may get our attention, but long term it doesn't gain our empathy. We don't see it as all that real."

- TO THE INTERRUPTER ("Folks tell me I interrupt them unnecessarily, but what I say is important."), say,

     "What you say has value. You're important. What others say has value. They're important. Everyone should have a chance to participate in the conversation without being interrupted."

- TO THE GRUMBLER ("When I don't get what I want, I'm unhappy and feel it's my right to gripe."), say,

     "At one level I feel honored that you'd include

me in your grievances, but honestly none of us has a perfect life, and it's more energizing to be grateful than resentful."

- TO THE DISTRACTOR ("I refuse to be put on the hot seat, so I sidetrack others with unrelated stuff."), say,

  "Until now I had assumed you and I had mutual respect, but you are evading my questions by continually changing the subject and rambling."

- TO THE LIMELIGHTER ("Other people are quiet or boring, so I take center stage with my interests."), say,

  "I love your storytelling. You entertain me. But surely there is something we have in common so we can have a two-way conversation."

- TO THE PILE-ON-ER ("When upset, I think of additional stuff and say it; it's not off topic to me."), say,

  "I know I fail you. We fail each other. But I don't keep reloading during our arguments. Let's try to stay on topic and address one thing at a time."

- TO THE UNPRAYERFUL ("Maybe I should wait quietly in prayer, but I feel they need to hear it now."), say,

  "You should talk to God about others before you talk to others about God. Ask Him for discernment about whether what you want to say is necessary. Perhaps you should serve more. You know, preach Jesus, and, if necessary, use words."

In Conclusion

You may be inclined to think that after discussing at length the importance of speaking truth at all times, and doing so with kindness, that "necessary" feels a little low on the totem pole of importance and something to not waste too much time worrying about right now. But before you continue to the next chapter and lose sight of this one, let me remind you again what Jesus said in Matthew 12:36–37: "But I tell you that *every careless word that people speak*, they shall give an accounting for it in the day of judgment. For by your words you will be justified, and by your words you will be condemned."

So whether you are a Pile-On-er, a Grumbler, a Loose Cannon, or any other label we just mentioned, remember Jesus' warning about "every careless word that people speak." Every word from your mouth counts. Every last one. According to our loving Lord, there is no backspace button in life.

CHAPTER 4

IS IT CLEAR?

Scriptural Meditation on Clear Speech

- 1 Corinthians 14:9—So also you, unless you utter by the tongue **speech that is clear,** how will it be known what is spoken? For you will be speaking into the air.
- Colossians 4:3-4—Praying at the same time for us as well . . . that I may **make it clear** in the way I ought to speak.
- 1 Timothy 1:7—**They do not understand** either what they are saying or the matters about which they make confident assertions.

- 1 Corinthians 1:12; 5:10; 10:19—Now **I mean this; I did not at all mean; What do I mean then?**
- 1 Corinthians 14:10-11—There are, perhaps, a great many kinds of languages in the world, and no kind is without meaning. **If then I do not know the meaning of the language,** I will be to the one who speaks a barbarian, and the one who speaks will be a barbarian to me.
- Ephesians 4:9—Now this expression, "He ascended," **what does it mean . . . ?**
- Hebrews 12:27—**This expression,** "Yet once more," **denotes . . .**
- Ecclesiastes 12:9—He pondered, **searched out** and arranged many proverbs.
- Ecclesiastes 12:10—To **write words of truth correctly.**
- Luke 1:3-4—It seemed fitting for me as well, having **investigated everything carefully** from the beginning, to **write it out for you in consecutive order,** most excellent Theophilus; so that you may **know the exact truth** about the things you have been taught.
- Acts 11:4—Proceeded to explain to them in **orderly sequence.**
- 1 Corinthians 1:17—**Not in cleverness of speech.**
- Ephesians 3:4—When you read you can **understand my insight.**
- 2 Peter 3:16—All his letters . . . in which are some things **hard to understand.**

- 2 Corinthians 1:13—For we write nothing else to you than **what you read and understand**.
- Deuteronomy 27:8—And you shall write **very clearly** all the words of this law (NIV).
- Mark 8:32—And He was **stating the matter plainly**.

Communicating What Is Clear

Is the communication clear to others? When a boy, I had a Dalmatian that I named Fire. He escaped from our yard, so I went through the neighborhood calling out, "Fire! Fire! Fire!" Mrs. Lintz came running to her front door yelling, "Where?" I shouted back, "I don't know." She said, "Where's the fire?" Again, "I don't know. I am looking for him." She asked, "Him? What are you talking about?" I told her my dog, Fire, was lost. Shortly thereafter she called my parents. We changed my dog's name to Flyer.

Is my communication clear to me? A fellow said, "I may not be funny or athletic or good looking or smart or talented . . . I forget where I am going with this."

Though we laugh, this represents the daily speech of some. They forget where they are going. We need to be clear in our own minds as to where we are headed in what we are saying; otherwise, those on the receiving end will be more confused. As pastors, we say, "If there is a mist in the pulpit, there's a fog in the pew."

Anthony Hope Hawkins commented, "Unless one is a genius, it is best to aim at being intelligible."[1] And even if one is a genius, one learns ways of communicating clearly to various groups. It is one thing to talk to a group of academics about what we do. It is something else when explaining to our grandmothers what we do. They may not grasp the academic side, but every expert comes up with examples that enable laity to understand at a certain level. A good-hearted genius is very sensitive about talking over the heads of others and making them feel stupid but uses his intelligence to come up with stories and analogies that paint a clear picture that an elementary student can appreciate.

The point I am making is that we can and must be clear based on the different audiences with whom we communicate. The truth another needs to know can and must be clear, and we can and must convey it kindly.

The Heart of Communicating What Is Clear

Clarity starts from our hearts. Proverbs 15:28 states, "The heart of the righteous ponders how to answer." We read in Proverbs 16:23, "The heart of the wise instructs his mouth and adds persuasiveness to his lips."

When our hearts aren't in it, we do not ponder or self-instruct. We lack a heart of diligence to be organized, specific, precise, articulate, and coherent. On the other hand, when it is in our hearts to communicate what is true, kind, and necessary, it will be in our hearts to communicate these clearly.

As I stated earlier, I practiced the first three of kindly speaking what was true and necessary but realized that not everyone understood me because I was not clear. I had to make a decision to figure out better ways to answer. I needed to teach myself how to persuade better than I had been.

When the people in our world are saying, "I did not quite understand your point. What exactly did you mean?" then we need to sharpen our skills related to clear communication.

The best of communicators fall short. I watched a famous editor ask a famous author, "What did you mean here in what you wrote?" The author then explained what he meant. The editor shot back, "Then why in the world didn't you say that?" That scene, which I observed from another room, stuck with me for decades.

If even a great communicator must keep improving his skill, what about the rest of us? Are we hazy communicators because we are lazy communicators? Do we need to work harder at being clear about what we mean? Do we need to put more of our hearts into this? We need to care enough to be clear.

The Golden Rule of Clear Communication

None of us likes it when people are unclear with us about what is true. We dislike wondering, *Did they mean to say that in such an unloving and disrespectful manner?* And, for those who ramble, we find ourselves frustrated trying to figure out what is the essential point they seek to make.

We get annoyed by hazy and lazy communicators. We do not favor those who lack the discipline to enunciate well, write legibly, and use grammar appropriately. We are taken aback when we realize had the person reread what he or she wrote before hitting send, this would not appear so unintelligent.

We do not enjoy having to keep asking, "What did you mean by what you just said? Where did this happen, and when? Who was involved? Why are we just now hearing about this, and how did this happen? You provided no reasons. How do you expect us to respond?" We expect others to think well enough to clearly answer the What, When, Where, Who, Why, and How.

But this raises the question: Do we have the same standard for ourselves?

Why Do We Communicate What Is Unclear?

Given you are committed to communicating what is true, kind, and necessary, do you have misunderstandings among family, friends, or anyone with whom you interact? We agree that some folks do not listen carefully, but the other side is that we do not communicate clearly. Why might that be? Consider the following list. Do any of these types strike a chord? If so, consider the commentary about the reason for lack of clarity.

THE UNAWARE: At times when conferring, I'm unconscious others don't know what I know.

THE MYSTICAL: I know what I mean. I just cannot say it.

THE SPIDERWEBBER: I start out on one topic, but this can trigger a web of unrelated points.

THE MISCONSTRUED: I didn't mean it as they interpreted it, but yeah, those were my words.

THE INCOMPLETE: Occasionally I leave out vital stuff since I fail to answer the five Ws and H.

THE WILLFULLY IGNORANT: I sometimes talk while knowing I'm uninformed or misinformed.

THE DISORGANIZED: I am not always well thought out and well organized.

THE SNOB: Others don't understand because they're stupid. It isn't me. I'm clear.

THE JOKESTER: I try to be funny, but others hear it as sarcasm and misunderstand.

THE UNEDITED: I confess. When snubbed, I react instead of calmly editing myself to be clear.

THE HASTY: Yes, sometimes I'm hard to follow. I talk too fast and make impulsive remarks.

THE FENCE SITTER: I do not land on either side of an issue to avoid trouble with both sides.

THE PROVOKED: When upset, I do react in ways that appear unreasonable and confusing.

THE INDECISIVE: Yes, when undecided, my delay leaves others uncertain about my wishes.

THE RELATIVIST: I'm unmoved by my contradictions. Truth is what I say it is at the moment.

THE HUMBLE: I don't wish to appear self-promoting, so I veil my competencies.

THE OVERLY SENSITIVE: Not wanting to hurt people, I hold back on what is clearly true.

THE INTONER: The words I speak are sincere and clear, but my stern tone puzzles people.

THE WEARY: I don't think or communicate well
   when I'm too tired, especially at night.
THE PANICKING: When terrified, I can go bananas
   and leave others unnerved and uncertain.
THE HYPOCRITE: Granted, my words ring hollow
   when my actions don't match my words.

The Unaware

I met with fifteen professionals to get their feedback on this book. I recorded the meeting and had the content transcribed. When I went back over the transcripts, I found myself amazed at what I had missed. Also, there were moments various people recommended I do this or that, and I could tell they thought I knew how to do this or that like I knew the back of my hand. I remember thinking when first hearing them, *I'm not sure I would know how to do what you are suggesting.* Interestingly, during that time, I didn't stop any of them and say, "I don't know what you are talking about, not exactly," or "That is unclear to me." We just continued talking. They were not aware that I did not know what they knew. They just assumed I knew what they knew. No one asked, "Emerson, we threw a lot of information at you, is there anything unclear?"

A friend of mine, a great negotiator and builder, would engage clients and people by talking about his proposal, but he did so in short spurts. He would then ask, "Does this make sense?" He would continually solicit feedback. When his projects cost tens of millions of dollars, and townships and organizations needed to sign off, he knew it was crucial never to assume the other was buying what he was selling, or understood what he was saying. Even when people said it made sense, he'd ask, "In what ways does this make sense for you?"

When we are talking to others, many will appear as though they know what we know, but because most of us are insecure and no one wishes to look stupid, few put themselves in a position to say, "I don't know what you are talking about." People will even nod their heads and the presenter can assume they are tracking and agreeing, while later learning it went over their heads. We were talking about multiplication and division, but they hadn't learned to add and subtract. Though everything we kindly communicate about multiplication and division is true and necessary, earlier we should have kindly communicated what was true and necessary about addition and subtraction. We got ahead of ourselves and confused the others.

Before hitting send, we must ask, *Is this person on the same page with me?* When I am unaware of another's ignorance but talk to that person as though he or she knows what I know, I will be unclear.

The Mystical

When we say, "I know what I mean; I just cannot say it," we really don't know what we mean. We think with words. If we do not have the words in our brains, then we do not know what we mean in our brains.

Admittedly, trying to figure out exactly what we feel or think takes reflection. We need to think about what we are thinking and feeling. For example, *Why am I depressed? Am I depressed mostly because my sick child has the flu, or am I depressed mostly over the fight I had with my spouse?* Sometimes we lose sight of what is bothering us most deeply. That differs from saying, "I know very clearly what is most deeply bothering me, but I find it impossible to tell anyone with any words whatsoever."

When we seek to inform, we either know the information or we do not. When we seek to persuade another, we either know the goal of our persuasion or we do not. When we seek to affect the heart of another with words of love, we either know what we wish to convey about our affection or we do not.

"But, Emerson, I can say what I mean, but it still comes out poorly." As long as you say what you mean, you are halfway there. Now you just need to develop the skill of communicating better what you mean. You need to organize your thoughts and communicate them in an orderly fashion.

Even the apostle Paul worked at conveying what he meant. We read comments such as "I mean this," or "I did not at all mean," or "What do I mean then?" (1 Cor. 1:12; 5:10; 10:19). He would explain in clear language.

He himself said in 1 Corinthians 14:9, "Unless you utter by the tongue speech *that is clear*, how will it be known what is spoken? For you will be speaking into the air." He even asked for prayer. To the Colossians he wrote, "Praying at the same time for us as well . . . that I may *make it clear in the way I ought to speak*" (Col. 4:3–4).

Never hit send on a communication in which you've written, "I know what I mean. I just can't say it." Figure it out first.

The Spiderwebber

People who spiderweb could be coherent and know exactly where they are headed in the conversation, but others may get lost.

I recall a woman, a good friend of ours, who loved to tell stories. And when six or eight couples would eat dinner at one of the homes, she'd launch into a story. What I found fascinating was that the women sat on the edge of their seats as she recounted what happened to her the day before. However, to others of us, she seemed all over the place. She was at the store, then saw an aged teacher she had in high school, which prompted a comment about her dislike for world history but also reminded her of her aging mother she had to talk to about going to the retirement center that had great medical care, which reminded her that a medical doctor worked there that she used to babysit, who still couldn't match his clothes, and that prompted her to ask, "Do you like this new outfit I have on?" As she talked, one thought triggered another thought that triggered another thought. Nothing was completed, and nothing seemed connected.

As I studied her, I realized she had a half-dozen points all dangling out there. Most of the women laughed at her humor while tracking with everything. In the meantime, the men sat dazed, and two were sleeping, and I think her husband was calling the retirement center to see if they had availability for him. But eventually, she connected all the important dots. Though some strings dangled, others were woven beautifully into a narrative that had us laughing.

Some Spiderwebbers are entertainers. If we are not in that camp, and find people asking, "Where exactly are you going with this?" then we need to control our thoughts. We need to keep whatever it is we wish to say to three simple points, especially when presenting content.

Preachers have always used three points because that's about all people can walk away with remembering, or follow in the first place. If we have additional points, hopefully they fall under one of the three. Good communicators make it as simple as possible not only to remember what we have said but to figure out where we are headed in the first place or what we just said. An old country preacher used to say, "I tell 'em what I'm gonna tell 'em. Then I tell 'em. Then I tell 'em what I told 'em."

In today's world, with easy and immediate access to so many outlets unloading information on us constantly, a single individual dumping out a ton of information with no apparent connection will be mostly ignored. The brain of the listener cannot process incoherence.

The Misconstrued

We have heard the expression, "Say what you mean, and mean what you say."

Sometimes in the heat of the moment we bark things we do not mean. We overstate. A husband yells, "Nobody could love you!" But he doesn't mean it. He means, "I don't like you right now because of your attitude. You are not lovable." He is hurt and mad. Of course, what wife does not personalize? Feeling very unloved, she retorts, "You hate me! You've always hated me. You have never loved me!" Things escalate from there.

The "never" and "always" expressions lead to trouble. During quarrels, it is best to refrain from these comments. These are thoughtless and tactless.

A wife told me, "I now understand that when I

mention a material thing (like a new car, a new home, a new appliance) he takes it to heart, and feels bad that he cannot *provide* me with everything I want. I explained to him that just because I remark about something, that doesn't mean that I *want* it, more likely, I just admire it."

We need to backtrack when we say things that are misconstrued. A woman introduced my daughter Joy with, "This is Joy. She's the one that does all the videos on the Internet and often doesn't care what she looks like." Joy responded, "What did you say?" The lady responded, "Oh, I didn't mean it that way." Because Joy has posted childhood pictures of herself, especially during those awkward junior high days when she wore braces and weighed more than was best, many have marveled at her transparency. Most everyone relates to her but don't dare do what she does since they lack the confidence. Regardless, this woman blurted out something without thinking. What she meant was more positive, but it sounded to all who heard her as a put-down on Joy.

One person wrote to me, "Before, I didn't really consider how [this person] would interpret what I said, just as long as I said what I was feeling. [Now] . . . I don't seem to shoot my mouth off as much anymore." She thinks before she speaks.

Just because we are well meaning is no reason to believe others know our meaning. If we find ourselves frequently saying, "I didn't mean it the way it sounds," then we need to work harder at being clearer. We are wasting a lot of emotional energy. Therefore, we need to ask ourselves before we speak, *What will this person hear when I say it this way?*

The Incomplete

Do people ask you questions like, "What or who are you talking about? Why are you talking about this? When and where did this happen? How do you expect me to respond?"

If so, you need to be clearer.

Rudyard Kipling had some good words of advice: "I keep six honest serving-men (They taught me all I knew); their names are What and Why and When and How and Where and Who."[2]

Early on, most of us learn about the 5Ws and H: Who, What, When, Where, Why, and How. Though we need not answer these in all communication, they serve as a great reminder and guide for being more comprehensive. When they are essential and we ignore them, we leave people scratching their heads.

For instance, we e-mail a fellow manager in another department, **Hey, Teresa, sometime in the next several days, I want to talk to you about David.** Well, there are two Davids in the two departments, so to whom do we refer? And who is responsible to set up the meeting in several days and when exactly in the next several days and where? And why the meeting? Is this a good or bad talk about this "David"? This e-mail doesn't answer the why, the who, or the when. Teresa is left to wonder what in the world is going on.

The five Ws and H remove confusion. If you take away anything from this section, apply the five Ws and H as a foundational blueprint in the communication trade.

The Willfully Ignorant

I learned of an aging professor who lectured for years based on certain research, but when new research countered his earlier findings, he willfully ignored these advances. Instead of changing his notes and learning the new information, he turned a blind eye to the changes in his field. It was too much work to correct his class presentations. He kept lecturing as he had for years, though he knew his students would be uninformed and misinformed because he chose to be.

In courts this is called willful blindness or contrived ignorance. For instance, to avoid legal liability one intentionally keeps himself ignorant of the facts. Those who subscribe to the tactic say, "Don't tell me the truth or facts. Leave me in ignorance so when asked by authorities I can honestly say, 'I don't know.'" Of course, judges and lawyers try to uncover if this person was seeking plausible deniability.

But there is another angle on knowing that we do not know. In political circles the rule of thumb is never admit a mistake or that you don't know something. Thus, keep talking in an interview to sound like an expert, all the while aware that you don't know. Feeling on the hot seat, and determined never to be wrong, but fully cognizant that the information is insufficient or incorrect, keep moving your lips, weaving and ducking as best as your polemical skills permit.

The same carries over in business. Leaders can find themselves uninformed or misinformed but maintain the appearance of being in the know with the right information. However, after leaving the meeting, heads roll. The CEO blurts out to aides, "Don't ever put me in that situation again."

I sometimes wonder why such people don't say, "I do not have the right information here. I have communicated incorrectly." Why is it that we say, "Honesty is the best policy" except when we think it is not?

If you don't know, don't hit send on information that gives the impression that you do know. This would be untruthful communication, and people will feel not only lied to but also confused about what is fact and what is fiction. It is better to say, "I will need to get back to you. I realize the information I have is insufficient." Of course, you need to get back to them when you have been updated correctly. The good news is that most people will give you more time to get caught up.

The Disorganized

Many times I have been unclear because I was inattentive, not sequenced, and incomplete. An editor said to me, "This is not well thought out. For example, your answers don't fit the questions." Another editor recommended I title my paragraphs since it would force me to clarify in my mind what my main point was with those sentences. All of us need to ask ourselves, *What am I trying to say here, and am I saying it?*

When writing a blog post, I like to ask myself three questions: *What is the issue? Why is this an issue? How is this issue resolved?* These help my brain get organized more quickly and think more comprehensively.

When writing an e-mail, I will number my points when I have more than one point. Numbering forces me to think through ahead of time the exact points but also lets the recipient clearly know there are several ideas.

On some stuff I write, Sarah tells me, "Read it out loud to yourself." Hearing what I read enables me to edit what sounds unclear. Sometimes I send it to others for feedback, asking, "Is this clear?" Usually, I let time pass on what I am communicating, stepping away from the content. This allows me to reread with fresh eyes. I am always amazed at what I didn't see when I first wrote out my thoughts.

When people e-mail me about their marriages, they can be emotional and overwhelmed. In that condition, they can jump right in to telling me their problems. However, sometimes it takes me a few minutes to figure out exactly what is the root issue that prompted them to write to me. I am uncertain what they want from me. They might start by saying, **We are under financial pressure like we've never experienced before, and I have health problems that add to our expenses. This is leading to a lot of arguments.** I am thinking, is this a question about poor budgeting that is causing quarrels and they want financial advice? Five paragraphs later (if there are paragraphs), they'll write, **Okay, the reason I am writing is that my spouse had an affair five years ago, and I am still struggling with forgiveness.** They should have said this up front in the e-mail, but some people just start writing (or talking) and expect the other person to organize their words. They expect the listener to read their minds. Since they know their main point, they expect the other person to know their main point.

When we communicate, we need to pause long enough to ask ourselves, *What is the big idea here?* State that up front, and stay on that point; otherwise, we confuse others and appear confused. Whatever it is that we intend to say is overpowered by our disorganization and incoherence.

Each of us must realize we can be like the preacher in the pulpit who started with the biblical text, departed from the text, and never returned to the text. As pastors, we all laugh because we have been guilty. We may have had a main point in mind. But when all is said and done, our thoughts were so scattered due to lack of preparation that we lost our way. And what is worse, people walk away asking, "What exactly was his point?" That response reminds me of the little boy who told the preacher, "When I get older and make money, I am going to give you some." The pastor thanked the boy and asked why. "Because my dad said you are the poorest preacher he has ever heard."

The Snob

Lost on a back road in Florida, a couple pulled to the side of the road where a farmer stood by his mailbox. "How do you get to Sanford?" the couple asked. The farmer replied, "My brother-in-law takes me." This couple can blame this farmer for being stupid or start again with, "That's great. When your brother-in-law takes you, what route does he take?"

When there is confusion, I try to refrain from attacking another for not listening carefully (which may be the case). Instead, I take a run at communicating again but more clearly. I am not worse for the wear, other than taking a little more time. After all, what good is it to display a condescending attitude toward another as though he or she is unintelligent?

In these incidents I put the onus on myself to improve my communication skills. This prevents me from feeling like a vulnerable victim to people's inattentiveness. Even if they are not fully listening, it is better for me to say, "I guess I wasn't clear. Let me run at this again. What I am trying to say is . . ." After I restate myself I might ask, "Does that make better sense?" This is just common sense, and that feedback reassures me that I was clearer. This is so simple to do, though it may take a couple more exchanges than I prefer.

Only the Snob says, "I am better and smarter than everyone else, and I am not repeating myself to people who should have listened in the first place." This attitude may explain why people aren't listening to us in the first place.

The Jokester

Some sarcasm is innocent and fun loving. Parents say, "Money isn't everything in life, but it keeps you in touch with us." But other sarcasm bites. An employee says to his superior, "I work this hard for forty hours to be this poor?" Does the other person hear the joking as funny or nasty?

Should we use sarcasm to make a point? Not if the other interprets it as a put-down. If the other interprets as hurtful something by which we intended no harm, we have been unclear. We have sent the wrong message. For instance, the manager says to a new employee who botched a sale with a customer, "I am trying to envision you with a personality." Soon after, the new worker quits.

Sarcasm is rarely an effective teaching technique. Instead, it offends, like when a family member says something obvious and we remark, "How clever, Sherlock. Who would have known?" When that family member deflates and expresses hurt, the jokester snaps back, "I am just joking. Can't you take a joke?" That's not clear when it doesn't feel like a laughing matter. It is no joke when the other feels he or she is a joke.

Perhaps one of the most common mistakes people realize they have made after hitting send is their sarcasm. Most recipients hear it as a put-down. We need to ask ourselves, *Though I think this remark is humorous, will the other person hear it as hurtful?*

The Greek word for sarcasm, *sarkazein*, means "to tear flesh like dogs." When people do not see us as truly joking in our sarcasm, they conclude it is a disguised insult. They believe the supposed humor cloaks a deep-seated criticism. Indeed, sarcasm rips their hearts more than a direct confrontation of the issue. It eats away at them. For this reason, when we are genuinely trying to be funny, we need to clarify that when we observe a person's spirit deflate.

The Unedited

What if we lived by this: when offended, write, read, edit, reread, edit, reread, wait, reread, edit, and then send. Too exhausting? Perhaps. But this process is vital when angry or offended.

Perhaps you've heard the expression, "I was so see, I couldn't mad straight." Actually, it is true. When we are really, really mad, we don't see straight, or at least pay attention to things as we should. This is readily observed when people are livid and shoot off an e-mail. They say things they do not mean and later regret. They overstate their case and conveniently leave out self-incriminating information. They attack the person instead of solely addressing the issue.

As I said earlier, and this bears repeating, the more we are upset by something, the wiser it is to let twenty-four hours pass before responding, during which time we review what we want to say. During heated moments, the potential for unclear communication increases, which runs the risk of creating worse problems.

Even when emotions are not running high, being slipshod sends the wrong message. For instance, how many of us receive an e-mail or letter with our names misspelled, and these from folks claiming to know us well? My name is Emerson, not Emmerson. My wife's name is Sarah, not Sara. These little differences make a huge difference in whether we feel they really know us.

I once received an e-mail that had brackets with the phrase [*insert name here*] at the top. No one had inserted my name, yet it was supposedly a *personal* note.

Or what about the time I received an official contract from an organization expressing delight to do business with me? In the cover letter the organization expressed how special I was to them. However, when I read the contract, someone else's name was there. This was a template, and they had forgotten to remove that name and insert mine. I no longer felt special.

Such mistakes as these can be innocent errors due to understandable distractions. One has too many forms to send out in a short period of time, and errors predictably occur. But frequently if one goes back, one might uncover something else. The office worker had just had a spat with another worker. Feeling hurt and offended, she took her eyes off the ball. Steaming about the unkind and untruthful remarks, the worker shoved my contract into the envelope and sent it without double-checking the spelling of my name or if my name was actually in the contract.

We may not be lazy people, but we can act lazy when hurt, offended, or angry. We do not reread and edit what we write.

Before hitting send, I need to get in tune with my feelings. Am I so mad right now that I cannot see straight? If so, predictably I will be slipshod. The more important the communication the less I can afford making glaring mistakes. I need to calm down, give it some time, and reread it when my hurt and anger is not controlling me and causing me to make regrettable blunders.

The Hasty

We all have heard commercials where the professional announcer who talks faster than an auctioneer goes through a list of warnings or restrictions on a product. He talks so fast we end up ignoring what is said.

People can hear four hundred words per minute. The brain can listen faster than the mouth can speak. But when there is constant fast talking, people eventually block out what is said. Pausing brings people back into focus.

If we are fast talkers, we need to slow down. Though our intensity helps us think better, that intensity causes us to verbalize as quickly. We blurt out stuff as it comes to mind, almost on impulse. Not only is it unclear, since it is disconnected, but we also end up saying things we ought not to say.

In the court of law, witnesses are coached on not being too hasty in what they talk about under oath. When nervous, they can get in a hurry and be overly eager to answer. In their haste, they are thoughtless. This confuses the jury or judge. This is why a witness is instructed to take his time and, if something is not understood, ask for a restatement of the question rather than start talking nervously.

In social media, do some of us hurry to express our opinions, for instance, on marriage with no prior study and analysis? Forget the facts, we'll espouse our opinion quickly, **Divorce the bum!** We declare this though we heard only three sentences from a wife about her supposedly abusive husband. Though we don't know her and haven't heard from the husband or the three teenage kids, what does that matter? We are using speedy fingers to make our unresearched editorial in two tweets. After all, who has time to be quiet, slow down, think, gather all the facts, pray, and then speak?

The only redeeming thing here is that few are paying attention to our narrow dogmatism when we declare, "Divorce the bum!" since they are fixated on espousing their own hallowed, but hollow, sound bites on some other topic.

The Fence Sitter

Do I have such a fear of conflict and rejection that I straddle the fence on issues? Am I willing to compromise what I personally believe in order to stay out of trouble? That won't work with two people who differ. We must make a choice. Lack of clarity is never permanent or permitted.

I remember laughing out loud when I first heard the phrase, *When you straddle a wooden fence, you're going to hurt yourself.* Let's think about the pain that results for us when we straddle the fence in business. Our affirming answers on both sides of the discussion among the staff enable us to stay away from taking sides for a period of time. We have been kept from trouble from our lack of clarity on what we feel is the right decision. In our memos we have been vague and ambiguous. However, with most differences like this, a vote is called for. We can no longer remain undecided and uncommitted. When both sides realize we have been ducking and weaving, they demand that we land on one side or the other of the fence. Unfortunately, because of our deceptive avoidance, neither side respects us very much. The very thing we sought to avoid, we end up causing.

As difficult as this is, we must choose the side that best reflects our convictions. This is tough, but we must do up front what we're going to end up doing later when a vote is called for. When we put off the inevitable, we put off people. In trying to make both sides happy by not being for one side and against the other, we make both sides unhappy with us for being crafty.

The Provoked

A wife e-mailed me:

> My husband says that I am hostile toward him and
> that my anger is uncontrolled. He calls me abusive.
> When we argue, my physical gestures are often
> aggressive, I speak quickly, loudly and dramatically.
> I sometimes use sarcasm and name-calling. He also
> feels that my anger is often unwarranted, and he
> never knows when I am going to "blow up." Much of
> this is true . . . He says he has avoided home in the
> past because he doesn't know what he's going to find
> when he gets there. Will I be happy, depressed, mad,
> or distant?

In her defense, she probably felt hurt and provoked.
But like her, when upset and offended, do we appear to
lose it emotionally to those around us? Do we appear
unpredictable and even irrational? Do the things we say
make little sense? After we communicate in an excitable
fashion, are things open to question? Do we leave others
in doubt about our character?

For instance, at the township meeting we feel ignored
as citizens and thus provoked because a decision has been
made to put a cell phone tower near our homes. Feeling
impotent to persuade the township to change their plans,

we threaten the council. "You leave me no other recourse than to sue you and, before that, start a recall of every one of you on this board." Of course, neither of these things happen subsequent to that evening's meeting. They are empty threats. But some at the meeting who are our close neighbors conclude that we intend to do both. When we do nothing, we leave them confused. Over time our neighbors see us as emotional and unreasonable when provoked by some injustice toward us. They know we feel indignant, but they see us as handling it poorly, even appearing uncontrolled and overreactionary. We are a bit too dramatic for them.

When we are slighted and hurt, do we hit send on a communication that causes others to see us as easily provoked and, eventually, as bad tempered and unreasonable?

The Indecisive

Decision-making can be tough if the decision is a permanent one. Should we take our beloved grandmothers off life support? All of us struggle with such decisions. But even here a decision needs to be made. We cannot leave the medical community in the dark. They need to know clearly our wishes.

What about marriage? The classic scene revolves around two people who have been dating for a year. She believes he is the one and wishes to marry him. He does not propose marriage, though he romantically loves her. She finds herself confused and frustrated. "If he loves me, why doesn't he propose?" His quietness and indecisiveness leave her completely baffled. Eventually she ends the relationship and starts dating another man who she then marries a couple of years later.

I have had both men and women tell me that they backed away, like this fellow. Getting cold feet, they delayed. Feeling confused, they confused the other person who eventually headed in another direction. One person told me that he has deep regrets in losing the woman he feels he should have married, but his unwillingness to make certain decisions left her unclear about the direction of the relationship, and she eventually married someone else.

On the other hand, I have coached men and women who have panicked over the thought that they were making a mistake to marry a certain person. I have had them weigh that person's godliness and wisdom and appeal to them. Two such people come to mind, both of whom are happily married today to their certain person after nearly thirty years of marriage.

I am not commenting on whether a person should or should not marry. Instead, I used these examples to show that procrastination, delay, and indecisiveness is not always a good thing.

I might go back to school.
I might join the YMCA.
I might do that budget with envelopes.
I might volunteer at the church.
I might put my name in for that promotion.
I might join that Bible study.
I might . . .

Our indecisiveness and do-nothing approach to life drive people nuts. Sometimes it's better to make a poorer decision and move things forward than to make no decision and leave people waiting and wondering.

The Relativist

Is truth relative? Not when it comes to the construction of our three-story home. Who hires a construction firm that adheres to the idea that the mathematical configurations about structural stress don't matter since truth is relative?

On college campuses some professors wax eloquent about truth always being relative. A student told me that he raised his hand in a class when one professor lectured that there were no absolute truths. He asked, "Prof, are you saying that rape is not always wrong?" That political hot potato triggered a class discussion that ended with the class—filled with women—believing in absolute truth. Some things are inherently evil, wrong, or false. It is always wrong to rape someone, and it is always wrong to say someone raped you when he, in fact, did not.

What is interesting is that most relativists wax eloquent about their relativism, but in their daily lives they hold firmly to certain beliefs in very dogmatic ways and end up contradicting their claim that there are no absolutes. They say one thing over here but live another way over there. Of course, they leave people confused about what they believe because of the glaring contradictions. Stephen Hicks illustrates this: "On the one hand, all truth is relative; on the other hand, postmodernism tells it like it really is. On the one hand, all cultures are equally deserving of respect; on the other, Western culture is uniquely destructive and bad. Values are subjective—but sexism and racism are really evil. Technology is bad and destructive—and it is unfair that some people have more technology than others. Tolerance is good and dominance is bad—but when postmodernists come to power, political correctness follows."[3]

When we contradict the very principles we espouse, the people who know us will say, "You can't have it both ways. Be clear. What do you really believe? Are you saying this out of selfish convenience or heartfelt conviction? Bald-headed men don't sell hair-restoration oil."

The Humble

Liz was vague about her desire for advancement because she did not wish to be viewed as prideful and self-promoting. She was not clear on her wishes and goals lest the CEO conclude she was self-serving and wrongly motivated.

Sadly, she had no intention about being unclear and misleading the CEO. Even so, her lack of clarity left the CEO in the dark about Liz's aspirations, so he gave the promotion to Sherry, who was unambiguous about her strong interests in the position. Later it came out about how much Liz wanted this position, and the CEO was in utter disbelief and deeply disappointed. He had concluded she was disinterested in the promotion.

Are you unclear because you seek to be humble but in the process mislead others? How can you let others know of your talents and passion while stating these things in a way that does not sound arrogant? Before not hitting send due to not wanting to be self-promoting, consult with some wise people in your life who can provide input on helping you convey your goals and desires without appearing boastful.

The Overly Sensitive

We all know the admonition "Speak the truth in love." However, some of us are so loving and sensitive that we withhold the necessary truth lest it hurt the person. We need to hear Proverbs 27:6: "Faithful are the wounds of a friend, but deceitful are the kisses of an enemy." When we care about the truth and care about the person, the most loving and respectful thing to do is speak clearly about what is necessary for that person to hear. Do we believe we are helping him or her by remaining silent?

Our coworker and friend believes a promotion is imminent, but we do not believe she has a remote chance for advancement. Perhaps we shouldn't say anything and let her hear the news on her own and deal with it on her own. But maybe we should say, "I am your friend, and I can be wrong, but my read is that your explosive anger in various staff meetings over the last year has removed you from the running. I do hope you get the promotion, but my gut tells me it is an uphill battle for you. And my desire is to be your friend and for you to begin addressing the anger issue so you don't sabotage future opportunities."

I talked with a mother of an adult son entertaining a divorce from his wife. She told me, "I am of a mind to go to his office and confront him." I urged her to do this. Because she was soft spoken and reserved, I told her that she of all people had a right to do this since her son knew that she rarely spoke this way, and her grandchildren needed their parents' marriage to remain intact.

Many times such people as this mother do not want to

make things worse and provoke the other person who is apt to act wounded, as though everyone is picking on him, and then claim, "That's the straw that broke the camel's back. I am finished with my wife and with this family. You pushed me over the edge!" That fear does something to sensitive people. They conjure up this worst-case scenario and so do not speak up. Somehow they feel they might be responsible for making things worse. But when is that ever the case? They need to see that their caring demeanor and words qualify them to speak up clearly and would never be viewed by objective people as the straw that broke the camel's back. Encouragingly, this son called off his divorce and is working on his marriage.

The Intoner

A wife asks, "Do you love me?" The husband replies, "Yes, of course." But the hesitancy and lack of passion say otherwise.

You've heard, "Don't look at me with that tone of voice!" I say at our marriage conferences, "You can be right but wrong at the top of your voice." When your inflection sounds contradictory to your words, those listening will be confused.

Some argue that a small percentage of conflicts are caused by the issue at hand, but the larger conflict becomes one of tones that sound unloving and disrespectful. People are left wondering, *What does this person really feel about me?*

We all know, or should know, that our tone of voice, the look in our eyes, the facial expressions, the posture of our bodies, and our proximity to the other person send a message far louder than the words we speak. When there is incongruity between the verbal ("I love you") and the nonverbal (never home), people will eventually interpret us through the nonverbal.

Is this why people are emoticon-ing their way through life? They want to make sure no one misunderstands their tone since their sincerely written words might be misinterpreted. I guess that is a good thing, but it also reinforces the lack of confidence we have that our words clearly convey our goodwill. How lamentable that we need the protection of a smiley face.

The Weary

When I was a pastor, we had board meetings that would run late into the evening, pushing 11:00 p.m. At that point, we most often called it quits for the night. We knew that our best thinking exited much earlier, and anger could more easily surface during heated debates.

Though believers are instructed not to let the sun set on their anger, there are moments when two people may not be able to resolve the issue that angers them before nightfall. As two mature people, agreeing to resume the discussion the next day often proves the better course to take. Minds are clearer, and so are the words.

If one claims to be a night person, then this applies to your morning. Each of us needs to get in tune with when we are at our best and when we are not. The best of communicators calls a time-out when tired and weary. It is one thing to put people to sleep by what we say; it is another to say things while we are half-asleep. We can be half as civil. Before hitting send, ask, *Am I tired? Can I hardly see to read? Finish this in the morning. Do not hit sin. I mean send.*

The Panicking

Several decades ago two other young men and I were sound asleep in a cabin in the middle of the woods in northern Wisconsin. It was late August, and we were there as part of a two-week wilderness program through my college. It was hot, so we slept shirtless in our sleeping bags. It was absolutely pitch black. I was on the lower bunk, another guy was on top, and the third was on a single bed.

About 1:00 a.m. a mouse dropped on my bare back. It took me a second to wake up and realize what it was and that it was moving across my back. In shock, I came up like a rocket and hit the bottom boards of the upper bunk. The jolt was so great that the fellow on top thought a bear had entered the cabin, so he screamed, "Bear!"

Like a madman, he leaped out of the upper bunk, swinging, and landed on the guy in the single bed, who in turn thought the bear was attacking him. To fend off the bear, he screamed and threw punches, hitting the guy who just landed on him. All of this took place within a few seconds. Total chaos and confusion.

The three of us ended up in the middle of the room in a heap with me yelling, "Quit swinging; it was a mouse on my back! There's no bear!" When all of this sunk in, we all started laughing, and then it hit us: we were a bunch of wimps.

That story has always reminded me of how chaotic and confusing things can become during a moment of panic. We can run around like a chicken with its head cut off, just as my two friends and I did.

Some of us have weekly crisis moments that aren't crisis moments. We are driving the kids to school and running late due to getting up late. At the third red light, we hit the steering wheel and yell, "I can't believe this! Nothing goes right for me!" We are dismayed as though the automatic lights are secret aliens who conspire against us. The two kids in the backseat, ages nine and eleven, look at each other in bewilderment. "Who is our dad?" We confuse them.

All of us need grace extended to us during times of true panic. Chaos reigns when a bomb goes off in an airport. But others of us are in panic and chaos mode without a threat. It's only a mouse, not a bear, and we end up scaring everyone around us.

Some of us hit send when panicked about this and that, which eventually makes us appear to be Chicken Little screaming, "The sky is falling!" We turn into the boy from Aesop's Fables who cried wolf too many times. We lose all credibility because others believe us to be alarmists.

The Hypocrite

"He told me that he loved me, but then he left me and hasn't called me in two months. I have not seen him since." This is the classic story of jilted love. The boyfriend said one thing but did another. The talk and walk didn't match.

The manager tells the employee, "Yes, come in. I have time to chat with you." But ten minutes into the chat the manager starts looking at his watch. The employee thinks, *Yeah, he said he had time to chat and seemed truly interested, but now he sends me the message that he could not care less.*

When we send mixed messages, people believe the one that feels most negative to them. Whatever we say to counter our actions, given our actions are the more negative, will not neutralize our unacceptable behavior. Hollow words do not override pathetic and painful actions. A person told me, "I had a client who consistently was telling me that his payments would be several months late, and then he'd add 'LOL' at the end of his e-mail. I called him, and I asked, 'Do you think this is funny? I'm not laughing out loud. You are four months late with your payment, and this is unacceptable.'" The client's "LOL" was hollow in light of defaulting on his payments.

There are individuals who make promises and consistently fail to follow through. When confronted with the fact that they say one thing and do another, they defend themselves with, "I intended to do it." In their way of thinking, as long as they intended to do it, they are okay. But those around them no longer feel that it is okay.

Before hitting send, I need to ask myself, *Am I trying to communicate something here that cannot nullify my former conduct? If so, what must I do instead of say?*

Why Should We Communicate What Is Clear?

Why be clear? We do not want people to misunderstand the truth, our kindness, and what is necessary for them to hear.

Because we love the truth, we will make sure the other clearly understands the truth, the whole truth, and nothing but the truth.

Because we need people to know our kind intentions, we will make sure they clearly know that we are seeking to be loving and respectful people as we relay this information.

Because we need to communicate what is necessary, we will make sure they clearly grasp the essentials that are vital for them to know.

The challenge is never to assume we are clear when we aren't. Some of us talk and write like Yogi Berra, who was famous for his muddled sayings, such as, "Things in the past are never as they used to be." "A nickel ain't worth a dime anymore." "You'll make some wrong mistakes along the way, but only the wrong survive;" and "I found good things always come in pairs of threes."[4]

What about you? Do you regularly hear, "I am not following you. . . . That doesn't make sense. . . . What exactly do you mean? . . . Can you go over that again? . . . I have no idea what you are saying. . . . You are losing me. . . . I am not getting your point."?

Most often communication breakdowns among people of goodwill are due to an honest misunderstanding. We are friends and allies. We are family members who trust one another. However, for the many reasons stated earlier about why we communicate unclearly, we have not worked hard enough at removing the possible confusion and misunderstanding. The incentive for working hard is simple enough: we want to communicate clearly because the truth matters, our kindness matters, and what is necessary matters.

How Can We Respond to Others Who Communicate What Is Unclear?

To start a conversation with another who has communicated unclearly, these statements could assist you in encouraging the other to be clearer.

- TO THE UNAWARE ("At times when conferring, I'm unconscious others don't know what I know."), say,

    "Unless you know to the contrary, don't assume I know what you know. To find out, ask me. After you start talking, ask if what you're saying makes sense. Help me along, okay?"
- TO THE MYSTICAL ("I know what I mean. I just cannot say it."), say,

    "When you can't say it, you don't know what you mean. And if you don't know what you mean, I definitely won't."

- TO THE SPIDERWEBBER ("I start out on one topic, but this can trigger a web of unrelated points."), say,

    "As you talk, your points seem barely connected. You go up, down, and around, and leave them dangling. Help me see where you're going. What's your main point?"

- TO THE MISCONSTRUED ("I didn't mean it as they interpreted it, but yeah, those were my words."), say,

    "Though I may have misunderstood what you meant, you did say what you said. So don't blame me or let your good intentions serve as an excuse to deny the impact of your words."

- TO THE INCOMPLETE ("Occasionally I leave out vital stuff since I fail to answer the five Ws and H."), say,

    "Please don't assume I know what you are talking about on this subject or that I know how or when to do what you request. Please help me by answering the five Ws and H."

- TO THE WILLFULLY IGNORANT ("I sometimes talk while knowing I'm uninformed or misinformed."), say,

    "Why would you consciously and willfully do this? Isn't that lying? Regardless of your reasons, you end up confusing and misleading me. Ignorance isn't bliss."

- TO THE DISORGANIZED ("I am not always well thought out and well organized."), say,

"I appreciate what you have to say when it is true and necessary but not in an unorganized and absentminded way. I'm interested in hearing you, but it's hard for me to keep track."

- TO THE SNOB ("Others don't understand because they're stupid. It isn't me. I'm clear."), say,

   "I'm not stupid for not understanding. You aren't being understandable or patient enough to help me understand."

- TO THE JOKESTER ("I try to be funny, but others hear it as sarcasm and misunderstand."), say,

   "Are you making me laugh or slyly making a point? You avow, 'I didn't mean it. Lighten up; it's a joke.' I can't. This is no joke. You're being wily not witty."

- TO THE UNEDITED ("I confess. When snubbed, I react instead of calmly editing myself to be clear."), say,

   "Unthinkingly barking out negative words definitely makes you appear unthinking! Jot down your thoughts first and take time to edit yourself. Give yourself twenty-four hours, okay?"

- TO THE HASTY ("Yes, sometimes I'm hard to follow. I talk too fast and make impulsive remarks."), say,

   "Speed walking is good. Speed talking is bad. What you say doesn't matter if I can't keep up with you. And some comments are made hastily without thinking, true?"

- TO THE FENCE SITTER ("I do not land on either side of an issue to avoid trouble with both sides."), say,

    "When you agree with me and with the person who disagrees with me, you are a fence sitter and frustrate us both."

- TO THE PROVOKED ("When upset, I do react in ways that appear unreasonable and confusing."), say,

    "When you are hurt or offended, you go haywire. Am I wrong? Your words unravel into a disorderly tangle, and you are momentarily out of control."

- TO THE INDECISIVE ("Yes, when undecided, my delay leaves others uncertain about my wishes."), say,

    "When you know the pros and cons but remain undecided, it confuses me. If postponement isn't an option, please come to a decision."

- TO THE RELATIVIST ("I'm unmoved by my contradictions. Truth is what I say it is at the moment."), say,

    "I need help to know your true convictions. You contradict yourself. For instance, you say there is no one right way of believing anything, and then you tell me there is a right way."

- TO THE HUMBLE ("I don't wish to appear self-promoting, so I veil my competencies."), say,

"When I need something accomplished and you know you can do it but don't tell me because you don't want to appear self-promoting, I am left in the dark, and we both lose out."

- TO THE OVERLY SENSITIVE ("Not wanting to hurt people, I hold back on what is clearly true."), say,

"It is one thing to speak the truth without love and another to be compassionate yet not truthful. In fearing you'll be hurtful, you're not helpful if you withhold the truth."

- TO THE INTONER ("The words I speak are sincere and clear, but my stern tone puzzles people."), say,

"Look, you can be clear and right in what you exclaim, but when you do it at the top of your voice in an unkind tone, you're sending another message."

- TO THE WEARY ("I don't think or communicate well when I'm too tired, especially at night."), say,

"Late-night talks work for night owls. You're an early bird. Wait until the morning to discuss stuff in depth and clearly. When you're ready to drop, drop the subject."

- TO THE PANICKING ("When terrified, I can go bananas and leave others unnerved and uncertain."), say,

"In crisis, there is panic. But a broken hangnail or honking driver isn't a disaster. In small matters, don't

---

wail like the sky is falling. You unnerve me and things feel chaotic."

- TO THE HYPOCRITE ("Granted, my words ring hollow when my actions don't match my words."), say,

  "You converse well enough, but then you look at your watch, tap your fingers nervously, and falsely smile. Your mind is elsewhere. I wonder if you've heard anything I've said."

In Conclusion

Words need to be well thought out and clear. For example, when we are on the receiving end of a communication, we cannot look into the eyes of an e-mail and see that it's joking. We cannot hear the innocent tone in a tweet. And Facebook doesn't yet have an automatic reply of **No, wait. That's not how I meant it** as soon as a reader interprets a post or comment the wrong way.

Oftentimes, others' perceptions behind our communications are just as important as our intentions behind what we were sharing. Though we may have spoken truthfully, with kindness and respect, and at the necessary time, if the communication is not perceived in the way we intended, then we must ask ourselves if we were as clear as we could have been.

The apostle Paul captured our goal in what he shared with the Corinthian church, "Unless you utter by the tongue speech that is clear, how will it be known what is spoken?" (1 Cor. 14:9).

AFTER YOU HIT SEND: WHY CONFESS OUR UNTRUE, UNKIND, UNNECESSARY, AND UNCLEAR STATEMENTS?

The wise King Solomon revealed these discerning words to us in Proverbs 6:2–3: "If you have been snared with the words of your mouth, have been caught with the words of your mouth, do this then, my son, and deliver yourself; since you have come into the hand of your neighbor, go, humble yourself, and importune your neighbor."

"But why, Emerson? Why must I confess these communication failings of mine? That's not how it was done in my family while growing up. We simply went to bed and started the next day all over, as though everything was okay. If I had been unkind, they knew I didn't mean to be. If I was unclear, they eventually figured it all out. Why do I need to revisit every untrue, unkind, unnecessary, and unclear word? Can't we just let it go? Besides, I don't see people apologizing on social media after tweeting lies about a political candidate, writing rudely about a spouse on Facebook, wrongly speculating about an investment opportunity for self-serving purposes, or being intentionally unclear in an e-mail to employees about future layoffs. Others don't say they are sorry, why should I?"

The answer for you is this: when you want to maintain the best possible relationship both with the one you offended as well as with God, you will make things right regardless of whether others do or do not and regardless of how things "worked" for your family while growing up.

Hear what Jesus had to say in Matthew 5:23–25: "If you are presenting your offering at the altar, and there remember that your brother has something against you, leave your offering there before the altar and go; first be reconciled to your brother, and then come and present your offering. Make friends quickly with your opponent."

Not only is Jesus telling us to put a same-day-delivery rush fee on any apologies or reconciliations that need to be made, even before we come to worship God, He is also making it clear that this reconciliation we need to seek out immediately is about the other person having something against us, not about whether he should or shouldn't feel this way. Even if we don't feel the other person is justified for having something against us, it is the better part of wisdom to go quickly and humbly to make things right. In these instances we need to err on the side of caution. And for those of us who know for a fact that we said something wrong and offensive, there is no other healthy recourse. Sweeping it under the rug is putting a land mine under the rug, which we will soon step on.

Though showing up quickly and humbly seems like too much work, it saves a whole lot of time and work later. The quick response averts the problem from surging and spiraling out of control. Acting quickly and humbly prevents the offense from taking root.

Do you need more reasons for why we must confess our untrue, unkind, unnecessary, and unclear words? Not that biblical commands, especially those from the mouth of Jesus, are not enough, but here are some other practical reasons that perhaps you may not have thought of.

IF THE ROLES WERE REVERSED, WE'D EXPECT
OTHERS TO CONFESS TO US. If others were mean to us,
lied to us, or were unclear in their communication to us,
resulting in hurt feelings and unnecessary turmoil, but
then denied their personal unresolved issues contributing to the problem, we'd be up in arms. We'd be saying,
"Wow, can't you at least humbly apologize for your part?"

Once again we go back to the Golden Rule, which
we have addressed in every chapter of this book. Just as
we should always ask ourselves before we speak, *Am I
about to communicate unto others in the way I would want
others to communicate unto me?* when we fail to do so and
in turn hurt someone, we should also ask ourselves, *If I
had been communicated to in the untrue, unkind, unnecessary, or unclear way that I have just communicated, would I
want the offender to apologize to me, the offended?*

The answer, most assuredly, would be yes.

CONFESSION TRIGGERS THE BEGINNING OF A
CHANGE. When we confess, what exactly are we doing?
Not to be formulistic about confession, but consider sev-
eral elements when doing so.

1. We confess that the way we spoke was wrong. "I
   was unkind," or "I did not exactly tell the whole
   truth in that e-mail." We must not try to make what
   we did appear okay or no big deal. It is best just to

say, "I was wrong for what I posted on Facebook." Wrong is wrong, as tough as that is to admit. But as we appreciate others who confess they were wrong, most folks will appreciate our maturity and humility.

2. We confess, "It was my fault." None of us can stand the person who apologizes but adds a ton of excuses. "I was unkind, but it's all your fault," or "I lied, but you couldn't handle the truth." How convenient to believe we are puppets on a string, controlled by others who are at fault for our wrong communications. But people see through that in a heartbeat. Remember, my response is my responsibility.

3. By the way, we need not apologize for what they did wrong, but neither do we bring up what they did wrong. During confession, we leave that to them; otherwise, they will think we confess to get them to confess. So, for instance, if the exchange turned heated and both were at fault 50/50, we own up to our 50 percent without saying a word about them owning up to their 50 percent. Similar to what was just said, their response is their responsibility.

4. We seek forgiveness. We ask, "Will you forgive me for copying the boss on that e-mail to you?" It isn't enough to tell others we are sorry. They could retort, "Who cares that you are sorry? What about

my feelings?" Asking for forgiveness, not demanding it, lets them know we care about what they feel. They are in the driver's seat on forgiveness. We are hoping they will forgive and allow for a new beginning since they are the ones who matter here. The offense came to them.

5. We state, "Here's what I will do differently to communicate better next time." The Bible teaches that there must be fruit in keeping with repentance. That's reasonable. We would expect people who confess to us to change course. If they confess to harsh or unnecessary speech but do nothing to change, the confession is pointless.

CONFESSION MAKES THINGS RIGHT BETWEEN GOD AND US. We who believe in God have heard the prayer of the psalmist, "Let the words of my mouth . . . be acceptable in Your sight, O LORD, my rock and my Redeemer" (Ps. 19:14). We know that our unlovingly untrue, unkind, unnecessary, and unclear words toward others affect God's heart. God loves us no matter what we speak, but that doesn't mean He approves or accepts every word we speak toward others. We know that when we sin against another, we also sin against God. When we confess to another, we need to also say, "Heavenly Father, forgive the words of my mouth."

In the end, both with God and with those we offended, we need to take ownership of our untrue, unkind, unnecessary, and unclear words. While there is no guarantee the offended party will accept our apology, confession is good for our souls, as they say. When we do what is right after communicating what was wrong, we clear our consciences and experience inner peace. So let me ask you four final questions:

1. *Do you need to go (write or call), quickly and humbly, to someone you may have offended?*

   When we arrogantly ignore people whom we caused to feel deeply hurt, frustrated, angry, fearful, confused, or offended, we will not remedy the problem. The problem will fester, and, given they have the opportunity, they will enact punitive consequences.

2. *Do you need to ask forgiveness from someone?*

   There are seven words I recommend that each of us speak: "I am sorry. Will you forgive me?" We may need to add, "How can I make this right by you?" Because we don't want people to harbor resentment toward us, we need to find out if they are willing to forgive us.

3. *Is there someone you need to reconcile with heart-to-heart and be on friendly terms with once again?*

This is the major goal with the other person. It isn't just to get through our confessions of wrong-doings so we can get out of there. It is to make friends, according to Jesus. This doesn't mean we become the best of friends. We can be the best of friends with only a few people, but we can be on friendly terms with most folks. As best as we can, we must ensure that this individual is no longer an offended opponent dead set on retaliation.

4. *Are you willing to seek reconciliation with another, if for no other reason than to please God?*

Those of us who are Christ-followers need to observe the deepest point Jesus makes in the Matthew 5 passage quoted at the beginning of this conclusion. Jesus reveals that we are at the altar before God, seeking to offer Him our best, when we realize our brother has something against us. To Jesus that relationship has to be restored so that our relationship with God can be enjoyed. So that we can be in God's presence with a clear conscience, the offended person in our lives takes precedence.

Sometimes we might find it necessary to write a note of apology as this woman did after she misspoke: "I am so

sorry for relaying my message to you in a very unnecessary and attackful way. Please forgive me and I ask that
you look past this and know that there is a lot on my
plate right now and that I was speaking out of frustration
because I am stressed. Please forgive my childish behavior. Will you?"

She made contact quickly and humbly. She entreated
the other to forgive her. She did this with the goal of recon-
ciling and being on friendly terms again. I also know she
did this because she knew her relationship with God
would not be what it could be until she made things
right. And asking the question allowed her to learn if the
other person did forgive, and allowed the other person to
forgive.

At the retail counter we raise our voices in complaint
and slam the clerk with a derogatory remark about the
company. Lickety-split, we change our tone. "I need
to apologize for that ugly comment. I was out of line.
Truly, I am sorry. You didn't deserve that. Will you forgive me?"

In an e-mail to a coworker, we blast him or her for
dropping the ball on a project. After hitting send, we
know we are out of line. As fast as our legs can carry us,
we head to that person's office to say, "Hey, I feel horrible
about the e-mail I just sent. I am out of line. You have
never said such things to me when I dropped the ball on

you, but you have been most gracious. I am a jerk. Will you forgive me?"

During dinner at home, we go off on a mouthy teenager and stop midstream and clamp down and say, "I was wrong for reacting this way, especially piling on with stuff that wasn't necessary for me to say. I am sorry. Will you forgive me? Then, let's focus on what troubles you."

In an e-mail to a few coworkers that started out as an invitation to a fantasy football league, we divulge information about another coworker who had a DUI and subsequently moved in with his mother because his wife kicked him out of the house. As others begin to respond, we feel it was not only wrong to disclose what we knew but our motive was also wrong; we were being vindictive because the person had not treated us kindly. Later we go in person to everyone who received the e-mail and apologize. "I was out of line for what I said. I need to ask you to forgive me."

Easy to do? Usually not. Is it the right and best thing to do? Always.

We know this is the right and best thing to do because we expect people to do this toward us when the roles are reversed. When we are offended, we do not want people to ignore us. We do not appreciate hearing, "Get over it." We can't stand it when they say, "Sorry," but could not care less about our feelings. On the other hand, our hearts are warmed when a person comes to us quickly and humbly to express sorrow and seek forgiveness, and asks us how he or she can make it right.

We are now back to the Golden Rule of true communication.

ACKNOWLEDGMENTS

I want to thank Joy Eggerichs Reed, my daughter and agent; and Matt Baugher, senior vice president and publisher of the W Publishing Group, for brainstorming on this idea of the book and Matt's brilliant title. Everyone loves this title, though the people who have known me as a pastor sometimes think I am saying, "Before You Hit Sin." There could be something to this.

My thanks to Kevin Harvey, who helped me edit the book and graciously served the reader by removing what was unnecessary and unclear.

For the final read of the manuscript, I am indebted to Paula Major, Karen Cole, and Joel Kneedler for their corrections and recommendations. This is detailed work. Thank you!

I wish to express my appreciation to the Thomas Nelson team of a dozen leaders who met for several hours with me to address the need of society to think before speaking. I am grateful for their rich suggestions. That was a delightful and inspiring time to me.

A special shout-out to my sister Ann who found several typos at the last hour. I enlisted my sister because there is no one better to correct me.

I am thankful for Sarah's love and respect for me while writing this book. She believes in me and the message of this book, and she sacrificed on many fronts to help make this happen. Thank you, Princess, especially for your prayers.

APPENDIX

Would you like to assess yourself?

In each of the four major categories—True, Kind, Necessary, and Clear—we have provided twenty principles. The principles in each category cluster into one of four or five broader groups. If you are interested in evaluating yourself on where you are strong and where you need to shore up your communication content and delivery, go to www.BeforeYouHitSend.org to take our survey.

In the category of Necessary communication, for example, you will answer questions like this one in the survey:

THE INTERRUPTER ("Folks tell me I interrupt them unnecessarily, but what I say is important.")

- ○ Very much like me
- ○ Somewhat like me
- ○ Neutral
- ○ Not much like me
- ○ Not at all like me

This falls into the Egocentric group. If you answered "Very much like me," it points toward you saying what is unnecessary because you are preoccupied with yourself and what is important only to you. But we don't conclude you are definitively egocentric unless you answer similarly to several other questions in this grouping.

For instance, another question would be:

THE PRYING ("Not knowing the details, I have to meddle to enable me to advance my cause.")

- ○ Very much like me
- ○ Somewhat like me
- ○ Neutral
- ○ Not much like me
- ○ Not at all like me

If you answered "Not much like me," perhaps Egocentric is not the group you fall into. It depends on how you answer the other questions in this cluster. Based on your answers, what unfolds is a helpful assessment of your communication strengths and challenges.

Again, go to www.BeforeYouHitSend.org for the tool, and you will receive several recommendations on how you can enhance your communications in a particular grouping.

Enjoy!

NOTES

Introduction

1. Ken Broda-Bahm, "Dance Like No One Is Watching; Email Like It May One Day Be Read Aloud in a Deposition," *Persuasive Litigator* (blog), July 28, 2016, www.persuasivelitigator.com/2016/07/dance-like-no-one-is-watching-email-like-it-may-one-day-be-read-aloud-in-a-deposition.html.

2. "By the Numbers: 73 Incredible Email Statistics," *DMR*, updated August 12, 2016, expandedramblings.com/index.php/email-statistics/.

3. "The Top 20 Valuable Facebook Statistics," Zephoria Inc., updated November 2016, https://zephoria.com/top-15-valuable-facebook-statistics/.

4. David Sayce, "10 Billions Tweets," accessed November 14, 2016, www.dsayce.com/social-media/10-billions-tweets/.

5. "13 People Who Got Fired for Tweeting," *Business Insider*, accessed November 14, 2016, www.businessinsider.com

/twitter-fired-2011-5?op=0#dont-tweet-bad-things-about
-your-potential-employer-1.

6. Jon Ronson, "How One Stupid Tweet Blew Up Justine Sacco's
   Life," *New York Times*, February 12, 2015, www.nytimes
   .com/2015/02/15/magazine/how-one-stupid-tweet-ruined
   -justine-saccos-life.html?_r=0.

7. Seth Godin, "Email Checklist," *Seth's Blog*, accessed
   November 14, 2016, sethgodin.typepad.com/seths_blog
   /2008/06/email-checklist.html.

8. *Socrates*, Essential Thinkers Series, Collector's Library (New
   York: Barnes and Noble Books, 2004).

9. In *The Children's Story Garden*. Stories collected by a
   committee of the Philadelphia Yearly Meeting—Anna Pettit
   Broomell, Emily Cooper Johnson, Elizabeth W. Collins, Alice
   Hall Paxson, Annie Hillborn, and Anna D. White. Illustrated
   by Katharine Richardson Wireman and Eugénie M. Wireman.
   Published in 1920 by J. B. Lippincott Company, Philadelphia.

10. Robert Fulghum, *All I Really Need to Know I Learned in
    Kindergarten* (New York: Villard Books, 1989).

11. James Clear, "Vince Lombardi on the Hidden Power of
    Mastering the Fundamentals," *James Clear* (blog), accessed
    November 14, 2006, jamesclear.com/vince-lombardi
    -fundamentals.

Chapter 1: Is It True?

1. Charles Dickens, *Great Expectations*, rev. ed. (New York:
   Penguin Classics, 2002), 71.

2. David H. Freedman, "Lies, Damned Lies, and Medical
   Science," *The Atlantic*, November 2010, www.theatlantic.com
   /magazine/archive/2010/11/lies-damned-lies-and-medical
   -science/308269/.

3. Abraham Lincoln, from a letter to George E. Pickett dated February 22, 1842, in Ida M. Tarbell, *The Life of Abraham Lincoln*, vol. 2 (New York: Cosimo, 2009), 277–78.

4. Elon Foster, *New Cyclopaedia of Prose Illustrations* (New York and London: Funk and Wagnalls, 1872), 355.

5. Kent Bach, "The Top 10 Misconceptions About Implicature," 2005, http://userwww.sfsu.edu/kbach/TopTen.pdf.

6. *Cycling News*, "Lance Armstrong Refutes Allegations," July 20, 1999, http://autobus.cyclingnews.com/results/1999/jul99/jul20.shtml.

7. In *Christian Teen Talk*, Chicken Soup for the Soul Series, "No, Really . . . Barney Ate My Report Card!" (New York: Chicken Soup for the Soul, 2008), 41.

8. Khaled Hosseini, *The Kite Runner* (New York: Riverhead Books, 2013), 18.

9. Eileen Ogintz, "Why Modern Millennial Vacations Are All About Bragging Rights," Fox News, July 29, 2016, www.foxnews.com/travel/2016/07/29/why-modern-millennial-vacations-are-all-about-bragging-rights.html.

10. Letter to John Bellows dated April 11, 1883, http://www.twainquotes.com/Lies.html.

11. Autobiographical dictation, December 2, 1906, published in *Autobiography of Mark Twain, Volume 2* (Oakland: University of California Press, 2013), http://www.twainquotes.com/Lies.html.

12. Benjamin Franklin, *Autobiography. Poor Richard. Letters.* (New York: D. Appleton, 1904), 246.

13. Meg Wagner, "Decade After Funeral, Woman Presumed Dead Talks About Mistaken ID," April 28, 2016, http://www.nydailynews.com/news/national/decade-funeral-woman-presumed-dead-talks-mistaken-id-article-1.2617753.

14. Dale Carnegie, *How to Win Friends and Influence People*, (New Orleans: Cornerstone Publishing, 2005), 129, images.kw.com /docs/2/1/2/212345/1285134779158_htwfaip.pdf.

15. Fyodor Dostoyevsky, *The Brothers Karamazov*, Book II: An Unfortunate Gathering, "The Old Buffoon," http://www .online-literature.com/dostoevsky/brothers_karamazov/7/.

16. William Shakespeare, *The Tragedy of Hamlet, Prince of Denmark*, act 1, scene 3, shakespeare.mit.edu/hamlet /hamlet.1.3.html.

17. Lauren Zander, "The Truth About People-Pleasers," *Huffington Post* (blog), October 20, 2015, www.huffingtonpost.com /lauren-zander/the-truth-about-peopleple_b_8333166.html.

18. K. W. Stout, "Confessions of a Former People Pleaser (and Why You Should Stop Being One)," *Health Mind Power*, January 22, 2015, healthmindpower.com/confessions -former-people-pleaser-stop-one/.

19. H. Mann, X. Garcia-Rada, D. Houser, and D. Ariely, "Everybody Else Is Doing It: Exploring Social Transmission of Lying Behavior," PLOS ONE, October 15, 2014, http:// journals.plos.org/plosone/article?id=10.1371/journal .pone.0109591.

20. *AskReddit*, November 20, 2012, https://www.reddit.com /r/AskReddit/comments/13i1m0/lies_beget_more_lies _once_you_start_lying_you/.

21. Pierre Corneille, *Le Menteur* (1644), act 3, scene 5, in *The Encarta Book of Quotations*, ed. by Bill Swainson (New York: St. Martin's Press, 2000), 233.

22. Vittorio Alfieri, *Virginia*, act 2, scene 3, in *Hoyt's New Cyclopedia of Practical Quotations* (New York: Funk and Wagnalls, 1922), 485.

23. Ralph Waldo Emerson, "The American Scholar," an address

at Harvard University, 1837, in *Emerson: Essays and Lectures* (New York: Library of America, 1983), 62.

24. "Weasel word," *Wikipedia*, updated January 8, 2017, https:// en.wikipedia.org/wiki/Weasel_word.

25. Isabel Fonseca, *Bury Me Standing: The Gypsies and Their Journey* (New York: Vintage, 1996), 15.

26. Theodore Roosevelt, *The New Nationalism* (New York: Outlook, 1910), 115–16.

27. Michael Josephson, "The Truth About Trust and Lies," *What Will Matter* (blog), accessed November 15, 2016, whatwillmatter.com/2016/09/truth-trust-lies/.

28. Plato, *Cratylus*, in *Plato in Twelve Volumes*, vol. 12, trans. Harold N. Fowler (Cambridge, MA: Harvard University Press, 1921), 435, www.perseus.tufts.edu/hopper/text?doc=Perseus %3Atext%3A1999.01.0172%3Atext%3DCrat.%3Apage%3 D435.

29. Mark Twain, *Mark Twain at Your Fingertips: A Book of Quotations*, comp. and ed. by Caroline Thomas Harnsberger (Mineola, New York: Dover Publications, 2009), 484.

30. Mark Twain, *The Adventures of Huckleberry Finn* (Seattle: Amazon Classics, 2015), 237.

Chapter 2: Is It Kind?

1. *Bambi*, directed by David Hand (Burbank, CA: Walt Disney Pictures, 1942).

2. Blake Skylar, "Do Social Networking Sites Create Anti-Social Behavior?" *People's World*, August 8, 2011, www.peoplesworld .org/article/do-social-networking-sites-create-anti-social -behavior/.

3. Luma Simms, "From Salem to DC: Mary Eberstadt's Analysis of the Dangerous Religion of Secular Progressivism," *The*

Public Discourse, Witherspoon Institute, June 28, 2016, www
.thepublicdiscourse.com/2016/06/17232.

4. George Eliot, *The Mill on the Floss* (n.p.: Eliot Press, 2013),
163.

5. Dietrich Bonhoeffer, *The Collected Sermons of Dietrich
Bonhoeffer* (Minneapolis: Fortress Press, 2012), 144.

6. Jeffrey Marlett, "Leo Durocher," Society for American
Baseball Research, accessed November 15, 2016, sabr.org
/bioproj/person/35d925c7.

7. Noel Sheppard, "Dr. Ben Carson Strikes Back at MSNBC's
Toure Neblett: I'm No Uncle Tom," MRC NewsBusters,
March 26, 2013, www.newsbusters.org/blogs/nb
/noel-sheppard/2013/03/26/dr-ben-carson-strikes-back
-msnbcs-toure-neblett-im-no-uncle-tom.

8. Charles Schulz, *Peanuts*, December 15, 1964, www.gocomics
.com/peanuts/1964/12/15.

9. Jon R. Stone, *The Routledge Book of World Proverbs* (New York:
Routledge, 2006), 129.

10. Martin Luther King Jr., "I Have a Dream," speech delivered
in 1963, in Eric J. Sundquist, *King's Dream* (New Haven: Yale
University Press, 2009), 14.

11. Martin Luther King Jr., *Strength to Love* (Minneapolis: Fortress
Press, 2010), 47.

12. Carol Harker, "Coach," *Iowa Alumni Magazine*, December
1989, www.iowalum.com/magazine/dec89/coach
.cfm?page=all.

13. Franklin D. Roosevelt: "Radio Address to the Young
Democratic Clubs of America," August 24, 1935, online by
Gerhard Peters and John T. Woolley, *The American Presidency
Project*, www.presidency.ucsb.edu/ws/?pid=14925.

14. Emily Post Quotations, The Emily Post Institute, accessed

November 15, 2016, http://emilypost.com/aboutemily
-postquotations.

15. Audrey Hepburn in "Audrey Hepburn, Many-Sided Charmer,"
    Life, December 7, 1953, 132, https://books.google.com
    /books?id=O0kEAAAAMBAJ&printsec=frontcover&source
    =gbs_ge_summary_r&cad=0#v=onepage&q&f=false.
16. George MacDonald, *Complete Works of George MacDonald*
    (Hastings, UK: Delphi Classics, 2015).
17. C. G. Jung, *The Collected Works of C. G. Jung: Complete
    Digital Edition* (Princeton: Princeton University Press, 2014),
    144.

Chapter 3: Is It Necessary?

1. Tiffany Bloodworth Rivers, "Tweets, Text and Chats, Oh My!
   5 Ways to Resist Workplace Distractions," *iOffice*, July 27,
   2017, https://www.iofficecorp.com/blog/tweets-text-and
   -chats-oh-my-five-ways-to-resist-workplace-distractions.
2. "How Do You Deal with People Who Dominate
   Conversation?" *Quora*, accessed November 15, 2016,
   https://www.quora.com/How-do-you-deal-with-people
   -who-dominate-conversation.
3. Kingsley Martin, "Winston Churchill Interviewed in 1939:
   'The British People Would Rather Go Down Fighting,'"
   New Statesmen, January 6, 2014, www.newstatesman.com
   /archive/2013/12/british-people-would-rather-go-down
   -fighting.

Chapter 4: Is It Clear?

1. Anthony Hope Hawkins, "A Very Fine Day," *Collected Works of
   Anthony Hope* (Hastings, UK: Delphi Publishing, 2016).
2. Rudyard Kipling, "I Keep Six Honest Serving Men," The

Kipling Society, accessed November 16, 2016, www
.kiplingsociety.co.uk/poems_serving.htm.

3. Stephen R. C. Hicks, *Explaining Postmodernism: Skepticism and Socialism from Rousseau to Foucault* (Tempe and New Berlin/Milwaukee: Scholargy Publishing, 2004), 184.

4. Dan O'Neill, "Yogi Berra's Commencement Address at St. Louis University," *St. Louis Post-Dispatch*, May 27, 2007.

ABOUT THE AUTHOR

Emerson Eggerichs, PhD, is an internationally known public speaker on the topic of male-female relationships and family dynamics. Dr. Eggerichs presents to live audiences around the country in his Love and Respect Conferences, based on more than three decades of counseling, as well as scientific and biblical research. This dynamic and life-changing conference is impacting the world, resulting in the healing and restoration of countless relationships.

Well-known as a dynamic speaker, Dr. Eggerichs has spoken to audiences across the spectrum, including NFL owners and coaches, PGA players and their spouses at the Players Championship, the New York Giants, the Miami Heat, members of Congress, and the Navy SEALs. But most honoring to him was being invited by the military brass to speak to troops in the Middle East.

Dr. Eggerichs has a BA in biblical studies from Wheaton College, an MA in communication from Wheaton College Graduate School, an MDiv from the University of Dubuque Theological Seminary, and a PhD in child and family ecology from Michigan State University. He has authored several books, including the *New York Times* bestseller *Love & Respect, Love & Respect in the Family*, and *Mother & Son*.

Before launching the Love and Respect Conferences, Dr. Eggerichs was the senior pastor of Trinity Church in Lansing, Michigan, for almost twenty years. Emerson and his wife, Sarah, have been married since 1973 and have three adult children. He is the founder and president of Love and Respect Ministries.

$\sim$

For more information, please visit
Love and Respect Ministries at

LoveandRespect.com.

You can also like the ministry on Facebook
and follow it on Twitter and Instagram

@Loverespectinc.